The Collegeville Prayer of the Faithful

General Intercessions for Years A, B, C

Michael Kwatera, O.S.B.

LITURGICAL PRESS
Collegeville, Minnesota

www.litpress.org

Nihil Obstat: Reverend Robert Harren, *Censor deputatus*
Imprimatur: ✠ Most Reverend John F. Kinney, J.C.D., D.D., Bishop of St. Cloud, Minnesota, May 26, 2009

Cover design by Monica Bokinskie

Excerpts from English translation of *The General Instruction of the Roman Missal* © 2002, International Committee on English in the Liturgy, Inc. (ICEL). All rights reserved.

© 2009 by Order of Saint Benedict, Collegeville, Minnesota. All rights reserved. No part of this book may be reproduced in any form, by print, microfilm, microfiche, mechanical recording, photocopying, translation, or by any other means, known or yet unknown, for any purpose except brief quotations in reviews, without the previous written permission of Liturgical Press, Saint John's Abbey, P.O. Box 7500, Collegeville, Minnesota 56321-7500. Printed in the United States of America.

Library of Congress Cataloging-in-Publication Data

Kwatera, Michael.
    The Collegeville prayer of the faithful : general intercessions for Years A, B, C / Michael Kwatera.
      p. cm.
    ISBN 978-0-8146-3282-6
    1. Church year—Prayers and devotions.   2. Common lectionary (1992) I. Title.

BV4812.K83 2009
264'.023—dc22   2009021207

Dedicated to

*my mother, Josephine Cecelia Kwatera (1917–2009),
and all who, like her, have received from the Lord
more than they can ask or imagine*

Contents

Introduction   ix

Year A

Advent   2

Christmas Season   10

Lent   24

Easter Triduum   38

Easter   44

Ordinary Time
    Second Sunday in Ordinary Time through
        Our Lord Jesus Christ the King   60

The Most Holy Trinity   126

The Most Holy Body and Blood of Christ   128

The Most Sacred Heart of Jesus   130

Dated Feasts and Civil Holidays
    The Immaculate Conception of the Blessed Virgin Mary   132
    Our Lady of Guadalupe   134
    Martin Luther King, Jr., Holiday   136
    St. Joseph, Husband of the Blessed Virgin Mary   138
    The Annunciation of the Lord   140
    Memorial Day   142
    The Nativity of St. John the Baptist   144
    Saint Peter and Saint Paul, Apostles   146

Independence Day   148
The Assumption of the Blessed Virgin Mary   150
Labor Day   152
The Exaltation of the Holy Cross   154
All Saints   156
All Souls   158
The Dedication of the Lateran Basilica in Rome   160
Thanksgiving Day   162

Year B

Advent   166

Christmas Season   174

Lent   188

Easter Triduum   202

Easter   208

Ordinary Time
   Second Sunday in Ordinary Time through
      Our Lord Jesus Christ the King   224

The Most Holy Trinity   290

The Most Holy Body and Blood of Christ   292

The Most Sacred Heart of Jesus   294

Dated Feasts and Civil Holidays
   The Immaculate Conception of the Blessed Virgin Mary   296
   Our Lady of Guadalupe   298
   Martin Luther King, Jr., Holiday   300
   St. Joseph, Husband of the Blessed Virgin Mary   302
   The Annunciation of the Lord   304
   Memorial Day   306
   The Nativity of St. John the Baptist   308
   Saint Peter and Saint Paul, Apostles   310
   Independence Day   312
   The Assumption of the Blessed Virgin Mary   314
   Labor Day   316
   The Exaltation of the Holy Cross   318

All Saints   320
All Souls   322
The Dedication of the Lateran Basilica in Rome   324
Thanksgiving Day   326

Year C

Advent   330

Christmas Season   338

Lent   352

Easter Triduum   366

Easter   372

Ordinary Time
  Second Sunday in Ordinary Time through
    Our Lord Jesus Christ the King   388

The Most Holy Trinity   454

The Most Holy Body and Blood of Christ   456

The Most Sacred Heart of Jesus   458

Dated Feasts and Civil Holidays
  The Immaculate Conception of the Blessed Virgin Mary   460
  Our Lady of Guadalupe   462
  Martin Luther King, Jr., Holiday   464
  St. Joseph, Husband of the Blessed Virgin Mary   466
  The Annunciation of the Lord   468
  Memorial Day   470
  The Nativity of St. John the Baptist   472
  Saint Peter and Saint Paul, Apostles   474
  Independence Day   476
  The Assumption of the Blessed Virgin Mary   478
  Labor Day   480
  The Exaltation of the Holy Cross   482
  All Saints   484
  All Souls   486
  The Dedication of the Lateran Basilica in Rome   488
  Thanksgiving Day   490

Introduction

When Pope Urban IV asked Thomas Aquinas to compose the Divine Office and Mass texts for the newly established feast of Corpus Christi (1264), the Dominican friar and theologian professed his unworthiness for so sacred a task. But he completed it beautifully. I am no Thomas Aquinas, yet I too feel humbled in preparing this collection of intercessory prayers for the eucharistic liturgy. To place prayerful words on human lips and in human hearts is a most sacred work.

My *Preparing the General Intercessions* (Liturgical Press, 1996) is a practical, "how-to" book for composing the prayer of the faithful for the Eucharist. This present volume is a collection of *almost* ready-to-pray intercessions for the Sundays, solemnities, and some civil holidays of the Lectionary's three-year cycle. I say "almost" because every liturgist and/or pastor will want to include particular persons and needs in the texts found here. Also, matters of immediate concern (for example, local tragedies and natural disasters) will need to be included in these rather general texts. Often the intentions can be made more "local" by changing the persons to be prayed for. While certain civil observances like Mother's Day and religious observances like World Mission Sunday are observed on fixed Sundays in particular months, they do not fall on the same Sundays of the liturgical calendar each year. Thus these observances cannot be indicated in the texts provided here. Liturgists will want to adapt these texts to reflect civil and religious observances throughout the year.

Preparing prayers for the Christian assembly to pray is a challenging but rewarding task. It took some courage for the Catholic Church to permit clergy and laypersons to prepare the prayer of the faithful for their congregations rather than legislating mandatory texts for use by the entire church. Thus, the *General Instruction of the Roman Missal* (2002) states:

> It is for the priest celebrant to direct this prayer from the chair. He himself begins it with a brief introduction, by which he invites the faithful to pray, and likewise he concludes it with a prayer. The intentions announced should be sober, be composed freely but prudently, and be succinct, and they should express the prayer of the entire community. (no. 71)

This statement gives generous freedom to those who prepare the prayer of the faithful but also requires careful discipline and theological accuracy in composing this prayer. I hope that such qualities are reflected in the prayer texts offered here.

Annie Dillard wrote about her Congregationalist pastor:

> Once, in the middle of the long pastoral prayer of intercession for the whole world—for the gift of wisdom to its leaders, for hope and mercy to the grieving and pained, succor to the oppressed, and God's grace to all—in the middle of this he stopped, and burst out, "Lord, we bring you these same petitions every week." After a shocked pause, he continued reading the prayer. Because of this, I like him very much.[1]

The church must pray for the same things every week, because the same human needs are old and new every Sunday in different persons. But these needs can be presented to God in fresh language shaped by the liturgical feasts, seasons, and the Sunday Scripture readings, as I have tried to do in this collection. Robert W. Hovda puts it very well: "The general intercessions are not there to impress the world with our knowledge of what is best for everybody. They are there to help worshipers rely more heavily on God's word and on God's Spirit than our own devices—or on the mass media."[2]

In preparing the intentions, I have searched the day's Scripture readings, and especially the responsorial psalm, for a word or phrase that leaps out from the text. Such a word or phrase has often been used in each of the intentions, repeated again and again as the series unfolds. This serves to link the prayer of the faithful to the prayer of the psalm. In this way, a pattern is developed that draws the worshipers into the intentions and provides a certain rhythmic, lyrical quality to them.

---

[1] Annie Dillard, *Holy the Firm* (New York: Harper & Row, 1977) 58–59.
[2] Robert W. Hovda, "Real and Worshipful Intercessions," *Worship* 60:6 (November 1986) 533.

As an example of this method, let us turn to the intentions for the Third Sunday of Advent (Year C) included here:

Minister: For leaders of Christian churches and communities,
that the Lord's strength
will renew them in their responsibilities,
let us pray to the Lord:

For leaders of governments,
that the Lord's courage
will lead them along the ways of justice and peace,
let us pray to the Lord:

For the sick and injured,
that the Lord's peace
will stand guard over their lives,
let us pray to the Lord:

For babies about to be born,
that the Lord's care
will bring them to the fullness of their humanity,
let us pray to the Lord:

For this assembly of God's people,
that the Lord's presence
will make us a source of spiritual joy for each other,
let us pray to the Lord:

For those who have died,
especially _____ and _____,
that the Lord's salvation
will fill them with everlasting joy,
let us pray to the Lord:

These intentions follow the order given in the *General Instruction of the Roman Missal* (2002):

    a. For the needs of the Church;
    b. For public authorities and the salvation of the whole world;
    c. For those burdened by any kind of difficulty;
    d. For the local community. (no. 70)

The pattern in these intentions is: For *someone*, that the Lord's *something* will *do something (something good!)* for them, let us pray to the Lord. Additions to this set of intercessions should follow this pattern for the sake of consistency. The pattern in each set of intentions should be easily discernible. This will be helpful as particular intentions are needed, for example, praying for first communicants and confirmation candidates, as well as for inviting the assembly to include their personal needs and intentions, if desired. Many of the sets of intentions in this book conclude with such an invitation. Presenting these additions in sense lines, as has been done in this book, will help lectors to proclaim these texts in the assembly.

Pope Benedict XVI has identified the intercessions as one of the liturgical "opportunities calling for the application of creativity."[3] Thus, the contribution of persons who have the gift of formulating intercessions should be encouraged. This task is properly the work of one gifted person for each occasion. "May he or she be a poet first," says Robert Hovda. "Any other qualifications are secondary."[4] Yes, a poet, because the Greek word "poet" means "creator." Preparing the prayer of the faithful is a craft in the service of the liturgy that requires divine assistance, human skill, and the fruitful creativity in which both work together.

Michael Kwatera, O.S.B.
June 29, 2009
Solemnity of SS. Peter and Paul, apostles

---

[3] Cardinal Joseph Ratzinger, "Structure of the Liturgical Celebration," in *The Feast of Faith: Approaches to a Theology of the Liturgy*, trans. Graham Harrison (San Francisco: Ignatius Press, 1986) 68.

[4] Robert W. Hovda, "The Prayer of General Intercession," *Worship* 44:8 (October 1970) 502.

Year A

FIRST SUNDAY OF ADVENT

Priest: As we begin the season of Advent,
we place our confidence in that glory begun in us
by Christ's first coming,
and claim the hope for that perfection to be accomplished in us
at his final coming.
May all people know Christ's many comings
in answer to these petitions.

Minister: That the leaders of the church will know Christ's coming
as they promote unity among Christians,
let us pray to the Lord:

That the leaders of nations will know Christ's coming
as they work to end oppression and violence,
let us pray to the Lord:

That the unemployed will know Christ's coming
as they find opportunities for fruitful work,
let us pray to the Lord:

That the sick,
especially _____ and _____,
will know Christ's coming
as they receive the kindness of their sisters and brothers,
let us pray to the Lord:

That we will know Christ's coming in one
    another
as we receive him in this Eucharist,
let us pray to the Lord:

That those who have died,
especially _____ and _____,
will know Christ's coming
as they celebrate life with him for ever,
let us pray to the Lord:

+

+

Priest: Lord God, your loving kindness enables us to
    find your Son
wherever he comes to us:
in his Word, in this meal, and in our brothers
    and sisters.
Let our prayers at this Eucharist
prepare us to welcome him at the end of time,
when he will be revealed as the Lord of glory,
for ever and ever. Amen.

SECOND SUNDAY OF ADVENT

Priest: The Lord Jesus is always near to us,
always coming into our hearts.
As we await the revelation of Christ's glory
at the end of the ages,
let us ask the Father to hear and answer the
 prayers we make
in the name of the beloved Son.

Minister: That the Lord will give wisdom
to those who shepherd and teach the church,
let us pray to the Lord:

That the Lord will give comfort
to those who live in the agony of warfare and
 violence,
let us pray to the Lord:

That the Lord will give healing
to those who are weakened by sickness,
especially _____ and _____,
let us pray to the Lord:

That the Lord will give perseverance
to those who are persecuted for their witness
 to the truth,
let us pray to the Lord:

That the Lord will give salvation
to those who have died,
especially _____ and _____,
let us pray to the Lord:

+

+

Priest: Lord God, ruler of all times and seasons,
we ask you to fill these days of waiting with
your saving love.
Help us grow in our love for you
and for each other,
and be at peace in your sight.
Bring us to glory with Jesus Christ,
who lives and reigns with you and the Holy
Spirit,
one God, for ever and ever. Amen.

THIRD SUNDAY OF ADVENT

Priest: My brothers and sisters,
let us rejoice heartily in the Lord Jesus Christ,
through whom the world was made in the beginning
and through whom it will be renewed
at the end of time.
Filled with confidence in God's promised salvation,
let us present these petitions
to the Giver of every blessing.

Minister: For Christian churches and communities,
that the Lord's glad tidings
will renew them in their words and deeds of discipleship,
let us pray to the Lord:

For leaders of governments,
that the Lord's glad tidings
will guide them in the ways of justice and peace,
let us pray to the Lord:

For the sick,
that the Lord's glad tidings
will heal them in mind and body,
let us pray to the Lord:

For babies about to be born,
that the Lord's glad tidings
will bring them to the fullness of their
    humanity,
let us pray to the Lord:

For this assembly of God's people,
that the Lord's glad tidings
will make us a source of spiritual joy for each
    other,
let us pray to the Lord:

For those who have died,
especially _____ and _____,
that the Lord's glad tidings
will be their everlasting joy,
let us pray to the Lord:

+

+

Priest: **Lord God,**
you have promised to renew all creation:
the world of nature and the world of the spirit.
Answer our prayers for enduring joy and
    gladness in Christ Jesus,
for he is near us now,
and will be with us in the world to come,
for ever and ever. Amen.

FOURTH SUNDAY OF ADVENT

Priest: My sisters and brothers, with Mary and Joseph
we know that all things are possible with God
and so we confidently ask the Lord to hear our prayers.

Minister: That the servants of Jesus Christ
will receive the Lord's blessing
in living the Gospel,
let us pray to the Lord:

That local, state, and national officials
will receive the Lord's blessing
in doing justice for all in need,
let us pray to the Lord:

That pregnant women
will receive the Lord's blessing
in the birth of their children,
let us pray to the Lord:

That those facing decisions about their future
will receive the Lord's blessing
in seeking God's will,
let us pray to the Lord:

That we who prepare to celebrate Christmas
will receive the Lord's blessing
in serving others,
let us pray to the Lord:

That those who have died,
especially _____ and _____,
will receive the Lord's blessing
in living with God for ever,
let us pray to the Lord:

+

+

Priest: God of Mary and Joseph, and our God,
we ask you to answer these prayers,
for we pray only that your will
be done in us and through us.
Let your blessing be powerfully present
in every word we speak and in every action
    we perform for your glory.
We ask this through Christ our Lord. Amen.

December 24

CHRISTMAS EVE

Priest: In deepest night, the light of God shines
  brightest
in our Savior, Christ the Lord.
Let us place our hope in him
as we pray in his name,
asking that God's salvation
will reach the ends of the earth.

Minister: That all members of the church
be renewed by the loving mercy of our God,
let us pray to the Lord:

That all who seek security or advantage
by means of violence
be converted to seeking the peace of our God,
let us pray to the Lord:

That unemployed, impoverished, and
  marginalized persons,
here in our midst and far away,
find deliverance in the justice of our God,
let us pray to the Lord:

That all who suffer from disease and injury,
especially _____ and _____,
know the healing love of our God,
let us pray to the Lord:

That all who worship here,
weighed down by the yoke of our sinfulness,
rejoice in the liberating power of our God,
let us pray to the Lord:

That those who have died,
especially _____ and _____,
live for ever in the radiant glory of our God,
let us pray to the Lord:

+

+

Priest: **God of glory,
we know your zeal for our salvation
in the birth of our Savior, Jesus Christ.
Let the grace we find in him
become the answer to our prayers,
this day and every day,
both now and for ever. Amen.**

December 25

CHRISTMAS DAY

Priest: This day our God came among us a tiny child
to show us the saving power of divine love.
Let us pray for the fullness of God's grace and truth
in ourselves and in all people,
even to the ends of the earth.

Minister: **That Jesus, Word of God made flesh,
be God's joy for all members of the church,
let us pray to the Lord:**

**That Jesus, desire of nations,
be God's peace among states and peoples,
let us pray to the Lord:**

**That Jesus, consolation of all hearts,
be God's healing and strength for those
in need,
let us pray to the Lord:**

**That Jesus, Savior of the world,
be God's light in our darkness,
let us pray to the Lord:**

**That Jesus, king of blessedness,
be God's everlasting happiness
for those who have died,
especially _____ and _____,
let us pray to the Lord:**

✢

✢

Priest: **Lord God,**
let your Son, born for us this day,
announce peace and good news to our world
in answer to these prayers.
Yours be the praise and the glory,
here on earth and in highest heaven,
both now and for ever. Amen.

THE HOLY FAMILY OF JESUS, MARY, AND JOSEPH

Priest: As we seek to walk together in the Lord's ways,
let us ask God's grace in all we say and do as God's family.

Minister: That all who are God's chosen ones by baptism
may be one in God's holy church,
let us pray to the Lord:

That all who fear the Lord,
of every nation and people,
may be one in their search for peace and justice,
let us pray to the Lord:

That Christian families may be one
in every virtue and mutual forgiveness,
let us pray to the Lord:

That all who are separated or estranged
from their relatives during this holy season
may be one in God's love,
let us pray to the Lord:

That those who have died,
especially _____ and _____,
may for ever be one in God's new Jerusalem,
let us pray to the Lord:

✢

✢

Priest: **Almighty Father,**
you sent your Son among us
to bring us your joy and peace.
Through these prayers, increase that joy
    and peace
in every human heart,
and multiply your blessings among us
for our good and your glory,
both now and for ever. Amen.

January 1

THE BLESSED VIRGIN MARY, THE MOTHER OF GOD

Priest: Through Jesus Christ, born of the Virgin Mary,
let us welcome the year of our Lord two thousand and _____
by turning to God in fervent prayer.

Minister: That those who serve the church
will know God's gracious love in their ministry,
let us pray to the Lord:

That leaders of governments
and all peoples of the earth
will know God's peace and justice in their communities,
let us pray to the Lord:

That those who face the future with anxiety
will know God's consolation in their fears,
let us pray to the Lord:

That we who are called to live as heirs of God
will know God's blessing in our lives,
let us pray to the Lord:

That those who have died,
especially _____ and _____,
will know God's salvation in their eternal home,
let us pray to the Lord:

    +

    +

Priest: **Lord our God,**
by the help of Mary's prayers,
keep us faithful in your service
during this new year that you give us,
and let our words and actions
give glory to your name.
We ask this through Christ our Lord. Amen.

SECOND SUNDAY AFTER CHRISTMAS
(where Epiphany is observed on January 6)

See also Year C, page 346.

Priest: As we give thanks for God's blessings,
let us offer our prayers for each other and for all in need.

Minister: That God's grace in Christ the Shepherd
will guide our Pope, our (arch) bishop, our pastor,
and all who serve our parish,
let us pray to the Lord:

That God's grace in Christ the peacemaker
will uphold world leaders and local officials
in their work for peace,
let us pray to the Lord:

That God's grace in Christ the liberator
will deliver those who are ill, hungry, or homeless,
let us pray to the Lord:

That God's grace in Christ the Savior
will enlighten us who worship here,
let us pray to the Lord:

That God's grace in Christ the life-giver
will raise those who have died,
especially _____ and _____,
to eternal joy,
let us pray to the Lord:

+

+

Priest: **Father,
grant us the riches of your grace
in answer to these prayers,
so that we will rejoice in your Son, Jesus
 Christ,
who dwells with us, both now and for ever.
 Amen.**

THE EPIPHANY OF THE LORD

Priest: Let us bring our prayers to the God of glory, who fulfills our hopes in the birth of the beloved Son.

Minister: That the church will announce God's salvation to the ends of the earth, let us pray to the Lord:

That the citizens of all nations will hallow God's name in peace, let us pray to the Lord:

That immigrants and exiles will rejoice in God's promise of justice and consolation, let us pray to the Lord:

That those weakened by sin and sickness will find strength in God's healing, let us pray to the Lord:

That we will show forth God's glory by lives of holiness, let us pray to the Lord:

That those who have died, especially _____ and _____, will know everlasting joy in proclaiming God's praise, let us pray to the Lord:

✢

✢

Priest: **Lord,**
we join with every nation to adore you,
for like the Magi, we find our everlasting light
    in your Son
who dwells with us.
Let his glory fill the earth
as his presence fills our lives.
Answer our prayers for your saving help,
and sustain us in your justice.
We ask this through Christ our Lord. Amen.

THE BAPTISM OF THE LORD

Priest: Gathered as God's holy people,
let us offer prayer for all in need,
both in this community and throughout all
 the world.

Minister: That the church, born of water and the Spirit,
may be filled with new power for good,
let us pray to the Lord:

That people of every nation
may be cleansed from hatred and violence,
let us pray to the Lord:

That those who suffer in body, mind, or spirit
may be freed from every evil,
let us pray to the Lord:

That we who form one people in Jesus Christ
may be made more perfectly like him,
let us pray to the Lord:

That those who have died
marked with the sign of faith,
especially _____ and _____,
may be reborn to eternal life,
let us pray to the Lord:

+

+

Priest: **Lord,
you empower those who have been baptized
to announce the good news of salvation
to people everywhere.
Hear and answer our prayers
to fulfill our baptismal mission,
so that all may live as your children,
brothers and sisters of Jesus Christ,
who is Lord for ever and ever. Amen.**

ASH WEDNESDAY

Priest: With trust in God's merciful love and faithful care,
let us present our needs in these prayers.

Minister: For the unity, peace, and welfare of the church of God
on its way to holy Easter,
let us pray to the Lord:

For the perseverance of those soon to receive the Easter sacraments,
let us pray to the Lord:

For the elimination of slavery, exploitation, and conflict
in human hearts and in our world,
let us pray to the Lord:

For the spiritual gifts we need
to fulfill our mission as ambassadors for Christ,
let us pray to the Lord:

For the grace to pray, fast, and serve the needy
as the Lord wills,
let us pray to the Lord:

For the happiness
of those called to share God's eternal day of salvation,
especially _____ and _____,
let us pray to the Lord:

　　　　　　　✝

　　　　　　　✝

Priest: **Giver of forgiveness,
hear our prayers for your merciful love
as we enter this season of repentance.
Let our fasting from sin
become our feasting on your Easter glory
in Jesus Christ,
who is Lord for ever and ever. Amen.**

FIRST SUNDAY OF LENT

Priest: In the spirit of Jesus,
who offered fervent prayer to his Father in the desert,
let us call upon the God of mercy.

Minister: That hesitation and doubt in those chosen today
for Christian initiation at Easter,
especially _____ and _____,
be taken away by God's faithfulness,
let us pray to the Lord:

That lukewarmness in our discipleship
be overcome by God's Holy Spirit,
let us pray to the Lord:

That poverty and injustice in this land and every land
be ended by God's compassion in human hearts,
let us pray to the Lord:

That the commitment of wives and husbands
be renewed by God's grace,
let us pray to the Lord:

That the death of our loved ones,
especially _____ and _____,
be turned into everlasting life by God's gift,
let us pray to the Lord:

+

+

Priest: **Lord God,**
you created Adam and Eve for your glory,
but they turned away from your love.
Now you have re-created us, their
 descendants,
through the obedience of your beloved Son.
In his name, we ask you to answer our
 prayers,
so that we may love you with all our hearts,
and do all that his Gospel requires of us.
Grant this through Christ our Lord. Amen.

SECOND SUNDAY OF LENT

Priest: Let us call upon the God of our ancestors, who is rich in compassion and love toward every generation.

Minister: That the Lord's mercy be upon the church and be its strength,
let us pray to the Lord:

That the Lord's mercy be upon candidates for reception into full communion of the Catholic Church especially _____ and _____,
and be their promise of salvation,
let us pray to the Lord:

That the Lord's mercy be upon nations and peoples,
especially the children of Abraham,
and be their source of justice and peace,
let us pray to the Lord:

That the Lord's mercy be upon all who are alienated from God and others,
and be their bond of love,
let us pray to the Lord:

That the Lord's mercy be upon us who are saved by Jesus Christ,
and be our hope in every difficulty,
let us pray to the Lord:

That the Lord's mercy be upon those who have died,
especially _____ and _____,
and be their gift of immortality,
let us pray to the Lord:

+

+

Priest: **Father of glory,**
you sent your beloved Son, Jesus Christ,
to redeem us from sin and lead us to holiness.
Answer our prayers,
so that we may receive your mercy
and share it with others.
We ask this through the same Christ our Lord.
Amen.

THIRD SUNDAY OF LENT

Priest: My sisters and brothers,
we are gathered during this holy season of repentance
to celebrate the mystery of our salvation in Jesus Christ.
Let us ask our merciful God to open for all the world
this fountain of life and blessing.

Minister: For all church leaders,
that their work be blessed and made fruitful,
let us pray to the Lord:

For those who are preparing for Christian initiation at Easter,
especially _____ and _____,
that they look forward to this celebration with fervent joy,
let us pray to the Lord:

For the leaders of our country and of every nation,
that they work together to meet the needs of the poor,
let us pray to the Lord:

For those who hunger and thirst for righteousness, justice, and peace,
that they be satisfied,
let us pray to the Lord:

For the ill, the aged, and the dying,
that their hope in God's merciful love
give them comfort and peace,
let us pray to the Lord:

For all of us who worship here,
that the love of God be abundantly poured
    into our hearts
so we may pour out that love to others,
let us pray to the Lord:

For those who have died,
especially _____ and _____,
that they rejoice for ever in the glory of God,
let us pray to the Lord:

+

+

Priest: **Lord God, you are our Savior.**
Let us draw water joyfully from the springs of
    your mercy
as did the woman of Samaria.
Grant us your saving help in answer to our
    prayers,
for we make them in the name of your Son,
Jesus Christ, who is Lord for ever and ever.
    Amen.

FOURTH SUNDAY OF LENT

Priest: Let us ask our God to illumine us and all the world
with the light of Christ
in answer to these prayers.

Minister: That all the members of the church,
and those who are preparing to become members at Easter,
especially _____ and _____,
will find renewed strength in God's mercy,
let us pray to the Lord:

That all people will find lasting peace in God's will,
let us pray to the Lord:

That the blind and the ill, the infirm and the dying,
will find abundant comfort in God's love,
let us pray to the Lord:

That all who worship here
will find welcome refreshment in God's goodness,
let us pray to the Lord:

That those who have died,
especially _____ and _____,
will find everlasting happiness in God's house,
let us pray to the Lord:

✢

✢

Priest: Lord God, unfailing light and Father of lights,
by the death and resurrection of Jesus Christ,
you have cast out the darkness of hatred and
    deceit,
and have poured out on the human family
the brightness of truth and love.
Answer the prayers we have made to you.
Help us to live as children of light,
this day and every day,
both now and for ever. Amen.

FIFTH SUNDAY OF LENT

Priest: Let us offer our fervent prayers to the living God,
who makes us fully alive in Christ Jesus.

Minister: That the ministers of the church
will know the Spirit's power in their self-sacrifice,
let us pray to the Lord:

That those who are preparing for baptism
[and for reception into the Catholic Church],
especially _____ and _____,
will know the Spirit's faithfulness
in their commitment to Christ,
let us pray to the Lord:

That the citizens of this and every land
will know the Spirit's peace
in their pursuit of justice,
let us pray to the Lord:

That we will know the Spirit's goodness
in our prayer, fasting, and works of charity,
let us pray to the Lord:

That those who have died,
especially _____ and _____,
will know the Spirit's joy in eternal life,
let us pray to the Lord:

✢

✢

Priest: **God of the living,
your Son raised Lazarus from death
as a sign that he came to give us life in fullest
 measure.
By your Holy Spirit, fill us with life.
Renew our faith, hope, and love,
so that we may live with you always,
and come to share the glory of the
 resurrection.
We ask this through Christ our Lord. Amen.**

PALM SUNDAY OF THE LORD'S PASSION

Priest: Jesus Christ suffered for us and left us an example
so that we could follow in his steps.
Let us ask God to guide our saving passage
through death to life
in answer to these prayers.

Minister: For all who bear Christ's name,
that they receive strength in the Lord
who endured the cross,
let us pray to the Lord:

For the elect and candidates for full communion,
especially _____ and _____,
that they receive joy
in knowing God's love and our love for them,
let us pray to the Lord:

For the people of this and every land,
that they receive the blessings of justice and peace,
let us pray to the Lord:

For the sick, the elderly, and the dying,
that they receive courage from the fidelity
of God's Suffering Servant,
let us pray to the Lord:

For us who enter upon this Holy Week,
that we receive salvation in confessing
that Jesus Christ is Lord,
let us pray to the Lord:

For those who have died,
especially _____ and _____,
that they receive everlasting glory
with their risen Savior,
let us pray to the Lord:

+

+

Priest: **Lord God,
by the precious and life-giving Cross of your
  beloved Son,
answer our prayers for the salvation we find
  in him.
Let it be our strength in your service,
this Sunday and this Holy Week,
both now and for ever. Amen.**

HOLY THURSDAY

Priest: Rejoicing in what we have received from the Lord—
a new and everlasting covenant in the Eucharist—
let us pray that this sacrifice of thanksgiving
will bring God's life to all the world.

Minister: That the Eucharist, sacrament of our passover with Christ,
will nourish the church during these most holy days,
let us pray to the Lord:

That the Eucharist, fount of all graces,
will lead all peoples and nations
to know and love Christ the Lord,
let us pray to the Lord:

That the Eucharist, fruit of suffering and death,
will console all who suffer,
especially _____ and _____,
let us pray to the Lord:

That the Eucharist, bread of life and cup of salvation,
will be our memorial feast of joy,
let us pray to the Lord:

That the Eucharist, food of travelers from this
    world to the next,
will raise up to everlasting life
those who have died,
especially _____ and _____,
let us pray to the Lord:

+

+

Priest: Liberating God,
receive these prayers
as we proclaim the death of your Son, Jesus
    Christ.
Answer them for the sake of him
who loved his own in this world even to
    death,
and who loves us, his sisters and brothers,
both now and for ever. Amen.

HOLY SATURDAY: EASTER VIGIL

Priest: Jesus Christ, risen from the dead,
has made us alive for God, now and always.
In his most sacred name,
let us pray that his glorious triumph over sin and death
will be ours in answer to these prayers.

Minister: That the holy and life-giving resurrection of Jesus
will bring glorious joy to all believers,
especially those who have been initiated
and received into the church this night,
_____ and _____,
let us pray to the Lord:

That the holy and life-giving resurrection of Jesus
will bring lasting justice and peace to the world,
let us pray to the Lord:

That the holy and life-giving resurrection of Jesus
will bring abundant healing and strength to all in need,
especially _____ and _____,
let us pray to the Lord:

That the holy and life-giving resurrection
 of Jesus
will bring renewed hope to us who worship
 here,
let us pray to the Lord:

That the holy and life-giving resurrection
 of Jesus
will bring eternal happiness to those who
 have died,
especially _____ and _____,
let us pray to the Lord:

+

+

Priest: **Wonderful in our eyes, O God,**
is the resurrection of your beloved Son.
Answer our prayers for the sake of him
who underwent the torment of the cross
but now reigns as the King of glory,
for ever and ever. Amen.

EASTER SUNDAY: THE RESURRECTION OF THE LORD

Priest: Christ Jesus, the source of our hope,
has been raised from the dead.
With thankful praise, let us offer these petitions.

Minister: For all who have been raised up with Christ in baptism,
especially _____ and _____,
that they rejoice in God's merciful love,
let us pray to the Lord:

For all who serve in public office,
that they rejoice in God's call for justice and peace,
let us pray to the Lord:

For those who suffer in body, mind, or spirit,
that they rejoice in God's deliverance,
let us pray to the Lord:

For this assembly,
that we rejoice in God's triumph over sin and death,
let us pray to the Lord:

For those who have died,
especially _____ and _____,
that they rejoice in God's gift of eternal life,
let us pray to the Lord:

            ✢

            ✢

Priest: **Most merciful God,**
your loving plan of salvation finds its glorious fulfillment
in the resurrection of your Son, Jesus Christ.
Extend that saving power
throughout our lives and our world,
this Easter day and every day,
both now and for ever. Amen.

SECOND SUNDAY OF EASTER
(Divine Mercy Sunday)

Priest: Wonderful in our eyes is the resurrection of Jesus,
the Son of God and minister of divine mercy.
Let us pray to share even now
in the eternal inheritance we have in him.

Minister: That those who preach the risen Christ in word and deed
receive strength in Jesus Christ,
let us pray to the Lord:

That those reborn at Easter,
especially _____ and _____,
receive joy in Jesus Christ,
let us pray to the Lord:

That all nations receive salvation in Jesus Christ,
let us pray to the Lord:

That all who are hard-pressed by sickness and injury,
by famine and warfare,
receive deliverance in Jesus Christ,
let us pray to the Lord:

That we who praise God this day
receive hope in Jesus Christ,
let us pray to the Lord:

That those who have died,
especially _____ and _____,
receive everlasting life in Jesus Christ,
let us pray to the Lord:

+

+

Priest: **Lord,**
we ask you to increase our faith in your risen
    Son,
so that we will welcome your salvation
in answer to these prayers.
Praise, glory, and honor be yours,
now and at the revelation of Jesus Christ,
who is Lord for ever and ever. Amen.

THIRD SUNDAY OF EASTER

Priest: When we are discouraged, God consoles us.
When we are troubled, God is with us to help us.
In grateful confidence, let us ask God to hear our petitions.

Minister: That the church will powerfully proclaim to all people
the hope which the risen Christ gives them,
let us pray to the Lord:

That Christ's message of peace
will remove the pain of war and violence from human hearts,
let us pray to the Lord:

That we will use the fruits of the earth
according to God's plan,
and thus help to restore all things in Christ,
let us pray to the Lord:

That we will recognize and give thanks to the risen Lord
in the breaking of the bread
and wherever he reveals himself,
let us pray to the Lord:

That those who have died,
especially _____ and _____,
will rejoice for ever in the glory of the risen Christ,
let us pray to the Lord:

+

+

Priest: **Father,**
truly your voice speaks of peace:
peace for us, your people,
and for all who turn to you in their hearts.
May our prayers at this Eucharist strengthen us
to be more worthy and grateful bearers of
your peace to others.
We ask this in the name of Jesus the Lord.
Amen.

FOURTH SUNDAY OF EASTER

Priest: With hearts filled with Easter joy,
let us bring our prayers to the God
who raised Jesus from the dead.

Minister: That those who shepherd the holy church
    of God
will find courage in the name of Jesus Christ,
let us pray to the Lord:

That those baptized at Easter,
especially our fellow parishioners,
_____ and _____,
will find lasting peace in the name of Jesus
    Christ,
let us pray to the Lord:

That those who are crushed by sadness, pain,
    and disappointment
will find joy in the name of Jesus Christ,
let us pray to the Lord:

That those who suffer from disability or
    injury
will find strength in the name of Jesus Christ,
let us pray to the Lord:

That those who lack sufficient food or
    adequate housing
will find bountiful help in the name of Jesus
    Christ,
let us pray to the Lord:

That those who have died,
especially _____ and _____,
will find eternal life in the name of Jesus
    Christ,
let us pray to the Lord:

+

+

Priest: **Lord God,
in the power of Jesus' name
we stand before you in fervent prayer.
Grant us and all your children
the salvation Christ won for us by his death
    and resurrection.
Keep us safe in his love,
and help us follow him to glory.
Let us dwell in your house,
at home with you, for ever and ever. Amen.**

FIFTH SUNDAY OF EASTER

Priest: In Christ Jesus, dead and risen,
we recognize the saving plan of God
and come to believe in the power of God's
    redeeming love.
With Easter faith,
let us present our prayers to the God of mercy.

Minister: That the Christian churches may persevere in
    faith
and bear witness to the unifying power of the
    Holy Spirit,
let us pray to the Lord:

That nations and peoples
may rejoice in the blessings of peace and
    justice,
let us pray to the Lord:

That our suffering sisters and brothers,
especially the sick of our parish,
may have their sorrow turned into lasting joy,
let us pray to the Lord:

That our parish community
may build up the spiritual temple of God in
    our midst,
let us pray to the Lord:

That all who have died,
especially _____ and _____,
may enjoy fullness of life with the risen
    Christ,
let us pray to the Lord:

+

+

Priest: Almighty God,
we thank you for calling us to be a holy
    people
in Jesus Christ, our way, our truth, and our life.
Hear the prayers we offer,
so that we may speak his words and do his
    works
for the salvation of all.
We ask this through the same Christ our Lord.
    Amen.

SIXTH SUNDAY OF EASTER

Priest: Jesus has not left us orphans,
for he has sent the Holy Spirit to be with us always.
Through the power of the Spirit,
let us give voice to the needs of people everywhere
in these petitions.

Minister: That the church may persevere in works of justice and peace,
let us pray to the Lord:

That those who govern and exercise authority
may bring hope to the nations of the world,
let us pray to the Lord:

That the hungry and the homeless
may know the presence of Jesus Christ,
let us pray to the Lord:

That all parents, especially single parents,
may receive the strength and power of the Spirit
as they care for their children,
let us pray to the Lord:

That those who have gone before us in death,
especially _____ and _____,
may enter the place Christ has prepared for them,
let us pray to the Lord:

+

+

Priest: We praise you, God of our joy, for your strong bond of love
which unites us to your risen Son.
Give us your Spirit to help us in all our needs,
so that we may love in deed and in truth.
We ask this through Christ our Lord. Amen.

ASCENSION OF THE LORD
(celebrated in some places on Sunday)

Priest: Our Lord Jesus Christ,
who took his seat at God's right hand,
remains with us and always works for our good.
In his name, let us pray for our needs
and the needs of all people.

Minister: That the victory of Jesus Christ over evil
will fill the church with his saving power,
let us pray to the Lord:

That the compassion of Jesus Christ
will fill the leaders of governments with his concern for others,
let us pray to the Lord:

That the presence of Jesus Christ
will fill the suffering with his consolation and strength,
let us pray to the Lord:

That the Gospel of Jesus Christ
will fill this assembly with his zeal for service,
let us pray to the Lord:

That the mercy of Jesus Christ will fill those who have died,
especially _____ and _____,
with his eternal glory,
let us pray to the Lord:

Let us remember our particular needs.

[pause for silent prayer]

That the grace of Jesus Christ
will fill our lives with his abundant gifts,
let us pray to the Lord:

+

+

Priest: Father most holy,
we ask you to hear our prayers,
so that in the time between Jesus' ascension
and his return in majesty,
we may bear witness to your everlasting love
  for us.
We ask this in the name of him
who has ascended to your right hand,
there to celebrate life with you and the Holy
  Spirit,
for ever and ever. Amen.

SEVENTH SUNDAY OF EASTER
(where the Ascension is celebrated on Thursday)

Priest: United in prayer with the Blessed Virgin Mary
and the apostles chosen by the Lord,
let us ask God for what we need this day.

Minister: For deeper faith in all the members of the church,
and for the support of those baptized at Easter,
especially _____ and _____,
let us pray to the Lord:

For the well-being of this nation and its government,
and for the safety of all who serve and protect us,
let us pray to the Lord:

For the comforting of those who suffer in body, mind, and spirit,
and for peace for the dying,
let us pray to the Lord:

For the continuing work of creation,
and for the building of a more humane world,
let us pray to the Lord:

For the ministry of God's care and healing to others at our hands,
and for abundant life in the reign of God,
let us pray to the Lord:

For eternal joy for the faithful departed,
especially _____ and _____,
and for consolation for all who mourn them,
let us pray to the Lord:

+

+

Priest: **Lord,
we ask to see your goodness in answer to
  these prayers.
Bring us to glory with Jesus Christ
in the land where all are alive for you,
for ever and ever. Amen.**

PENTECOST SUNDAY

Priest: United in the Spirit who helps us to pray rightly,
let us ask God to renew us and the face of the earth
in answer to these prayers.

Minister: May the glory of the Lord
be seen in the mutual service of God's people.
For this, let us pray to the Lord:

May the glory of the Lord
be seen in justice and peace among all nations.
For this, let us pray to the Lord:

May the glory of the Lord
be seen in the dedication and care of parents for their children.
For this, let us pray to the Lord:

May the glory of the Lord
be seen in healing for the sick,
especially _____ and _____,
and in recovery for the injured,
especially _____ and _____.
For this, let us pray to the Lord:

May the glory of the Lord
be seen in our faith, hope, and love.
For this, let us pray to the Lord:

May the glory of the Lord
be seen in everlasting happiness
for those who have died,
especially _____ and _____.
For this, let us pray to the Lord:

+

+

Priest: God of glory, giver of all good gifts,
mercifully answer our prayers.
Grant that we may welcome your Holy Spirit,
and rejoice to proclaim, "Jesus is Lord,"
both now and for ever. Amen.

SECOND SUNDAY IN ORDINARY TIME

Priest: The love of God embraces all peoples;
God's kindness knows no limit.
Let us place our hope in God
as we offer these petitions.

Minister: For the shepherds and guardians of the church,
let us pray to the Lord:

For those who work for the unity of all Christians,
let us pray to the Lord:

For those who are considering an abortion,
let us pray to the Lord:

For those who defend the sanctity of human life,
let us pray to the Lord:

For all who are hungry, homeless, or exploited by the powerful of this world,
let us pray to the Lord:

For our relatives and friends who are ill,
let us pray to the Lord:

For those who are dying
with no one to comfort them,
let us pray to the Lord:

For those who have died in the peace of Christ, especially _____ and _____,
let us pray to the Lord:

+

+

Priest: God of our strength, hear our prayers.
May our oneness with you and each other
be the living sign of your presence
in our divided world.
We ask this through Christ our Lord. Amen.

THIRD SUNDAY IN ORDINARY TIME

Priest: Let us turn to God in our need,
trusting in God's goodness and mercy.

Minister: For the leaders of the churches,
that they help all Christians to bear the fruit
    of the Spirit
in unity and love,
let us pray to the Lord:

For President _____ and
    Vice-President _____,
for members of the Cabinet and the Congress,
and for the justices of the Supreme Court,
that they protect the rights of all people,
let us pray to the Lord:

For expectant parents,
that they receive abundant strength and joy
in God's gift of life,
let us pray to the Lord:

For ourselves,
that we live in the light of the risen Christ
and accept his call to follow him,
let us pray to the Lord:

For those who have died,
especially _____ and _____,
that they celebrate everlasting life
with the Creator and Redeemer of all,
let us pray to the Lord:

+

+

Priest: God of the living,
you have called us to walk the way of unity
    and peace.
Confirm us in our hope that life is mightier
    than death,
and, in answer to our prayers,
let us know the great power for good
that flows from your Son's resurrection.
We ask this through Christ our Lord. Amen.

FOURTH SUNDAY IN ORDINARY TIME

Priest: Let us humbly take refuge in the name of the Lord
as we offer our petitions.

Minister: That Jesus, the wisdom of God,
will enlighten the church for proclaiming the reign of God,
let us pray to the Lord:

That Jesus, the righteousness of God,
will guide world leaders into the ways of peace and justice,
let us pray to the Lord:

That Jesus, the consolation of God,
will raise up the needy by our care for them,
let us pray to the Lord:

That Jesus, the sanctification of God,
will make us holy and blessed in doing God's will,
let us pray to the Lord:

That Jesus, the salvation of God,
will welcome the dead into his kingdom,
especially _____ and _____,
let us pray to the Lord:

✢

✢

Priest: **Ever-faithful God,**
we seek you in the midst of this assembly
and in the heart of our world.
As we call upon your name in these prayers,
answer them for the sake of your beloved Son,
Jesus Christ,
who is Lord for ever and ever. Amen.

FIFTH SUNDAY IN ORDINARY TIME

Priest: Faith is God's gift to those who doubt,
courage to those who are afraid,
and strength to those who are weak.
Let us ask God to hear these petitions.

Minister: That the church will receive the wisdom of Jesus
in its witness to the Gospel,
let us pray to the Lord:

That public officials will receive the power of Jesus
in their defense of human rights,
let us pray to the Lord:

That the people of our (arch)diocese
will receive the love of Jesus in their need,
let us pray to the Lord:

That we who celebrate this Eucharist
will receive the light of Jesus in our life of faith,
let us pray to the Lord:

That those who have died,
especially _____ and _____,
will receive the glory of Jesus in heaven,
let us pray to the Lord:

✢

✢

Priest: Father, trusting in your goodness,
we ask you to answer our prayers.
Come to our help,
so that the living flame of love in the heart of
 Jesus
and in our hearts will brighten our world.
We ask this through Christ our Lord. Amen.

SIXTH SUNDAY IN ORDINARY TIME

Priest: In the power of the Holy Spirit,
let us turn to God in confident prayer.

Minister: That God's goodness will be a source of wisdom
for all the members of the church,
let us pray to the Lord:

That God's goodness will be a source of peace
for nations and peoples,
let us pray to the Lord:

That God's will be a source of comfort
for those who suffer in mind or body,
let us pray to the Lord:

That God's goodness will be a source of holiness
for us as we walk in the way of the Lord,
let us pray to the Lord:

That God's goodness will be a source of everlasting life
for those who have died,
especially _____ and _____,
let us pray to the Lord:

+

+

Priest: God of wisdom and love,
you understand our every need even before
we ask.
Show us your goodness in answer to these
prayers,
so that keeping your commandments may be
our joy.
We ask this through Christ our Lord. Amen.

SEVENTH SUNDAY IN ORDINARY TIME

Priest: Let us present our prayers to the Lord,
whose kindness and mercy are our hope.

Minister: That the members of the church
will find renewed strength in God's love,
let us pray to the Lord:

That all nations and people
will find lasting peace in God's plan for this
world,
let us pray to the Lord:

That the ill and the infirm
will find abundant comfort in God's healing,
let us pray to the Lord:

That all who worship here
will find sure guidance in God's wisdom,
let us pray to the Lord:

That those who have died,
especially _____ and _____,
will find everlasting joy in God's glory,
let us pray to the Lord:

    +

    +

Priest: **All-holy God,**
we ask you to answer our prayers,
for you are merciful and gracious to all your people.
Rescue us from whatever could harm us,
and crown us with your kindness and compassion in Christ Jesus,
both now and for ever. Amen.

EIGHTH SUNDAY IN ORDINARY TIME

Priest: From God alone comes our salvation.
Let us pour out our hearts before the Lord in fervent prayer.

Minister: For the unity of the servants of Christ,
and for a life-giving share in the mysteries of God,
let us pray to the Lord:

For peace throughout the whole world,
and for the well-being of the human family,
let us pray to the Lord:

For an end to every threat to human life,
and for the elimination of hunger and disease,
let us pray to the Lord:

For the recovery of the sick,
and the relief of the poor,
let us pray to the Lord:

For the consolation of the dying,
and eternal life for those who have died,
especially _____ and _____,
let us pray to the Lord:

+

+

Priest: Rock of our strength,
you never forsake your people,
but remember them in your great love.
We place our trust in you,
and ask your generous blessings in Christ
 Jesus,
both now and for ever. Amen.

NINTH SUNDAY IN ORDINARY TIME

Priest: Let us bring our prayers to the Lord,
who leads us and guides us on the way of salvation.

Minister: That all who are justified by faith in Christ
will receive God's blessing in renewed hope,
let us pray to the Lord:

That all nations and communities
will receive God's blessing in lasting peace,
let us pray to the Lord:

That all who face difficult situations
will receive God's blessing in speedy deliverance,
let us pray to the Lord:

That we who celebrate the Eucharist here
will receive God's blessing in faithful love,
let us pray to the Lord:

That those who have died,
especially _____ and _____,
will receive God's blessing in everlasting joy,
let us pray to the Lord:

+

+

Priest: Lord, we call upon you,
our Rock of safety in every age.
Answer our prayers for your abundant
　　blessings in Christ Jesus,
both now and for ever. Amen.

TENTH SUNDAY IN ORDINARY TIME

Priest: Let us pray for our needs
and the needs of people everywhere.

Minister: That the saving power of God
will strengthen the church for words and
deeds of reconciliation,
let us pray to the Lord:

That the saving power of God
will draw nations and peoples to works of
justice and peace,
let us pray to the Lord:

That the saving power of God
will rescue the sick and the poor from their
distress,
let us pray to the Lord:

That the saving power of God
will remove from our lives whatever is
harmful
and give us whatever is helpful,
let us pray to the Lord:

That the saving power of God
will bring those who have died,
especially _____ and _____,
to the glory of the resurrection,
let us pray to the Lord:

+

+

Priest: Lord, like the apostle Matthew,
we find a welcome place at this table
with your Son, Jesus Christ.
In his most sacred name, we ask your
   promised help
in answer to these prayers,
so that your saving power may be ours,
both now and for ever. Amen.

ELEVENTH SUNDAY IN ORDINARY TIME

Priest: Jesus Christ loved us and gave himself up for us,
so that we might be put right with God.
Let us pray for ourselves and for all people.

Minister: That the leaders of the church will live for God
by seeking the unity of all Christians,
let us pray to the Lord:

That the nations and peoples of the earth will live for God
by embracing justice and peace,
let us pray to the Lord:

That husbands and wives will live for God
by generously serving their families in love,
let us pray to the Lord:

That those oppressed by any need will live for God
by believing firmly in Jesus Christ,
let us pray to the Lord:

That we who worship here will live for God
by forgiving each other from our hearts,
let us pray to the Lord:

That all who have died,
especially _____ and _____,
will live for God
by sharing in Christ's resurrection,
let us pray to the Lord:

+

+

Priest: Lord, though we are sinners,
you have taken away our guilt.
Shelter us and all people in answer to our
    prayers,
so that we may rejoice in you,
both now and for ever. Amen.

TWELFTH SUNDAY IN ORDINARY TIME

Priest: Let us ask God for what we need this day and this week
as we present these petitions.

Minister: For all who believe in Christ,
that God's loving favor will be theirs,
let us pray to the Lord:

For people of all nations,
that God's infinite mercy will be theirs,
let us pray to the Lord:

For the poor,
that God's bountiful help will be theirs at our hands,
let us pray to the Lord:

For all who suffer,
that God's abundant kindness will be theirs,
let us pray to the Lord:

For travelers and vacationers,
that God's constant protection will be theirs,
let us pray to the Lord:

For ourselves,
that God's enduring strength will be ours,
let us pray to the Lord:

For those who have died,
especially _____ and _____,
that God's everlasting love will be theirs,
let us pray to the Lord:

+

+

Priest: **Lord,
with the prophet Jeremiah
we entrust our lives into your hands.
With Jesus your Son,
we place our trust in your care for us.
Let your grace overflow for us and for all
 people
in answer to these prayers,
for we offer them in the name of Jesus Christ,
who is Lord for ever and ever. Amen.**

THIRTEENTH SUNDAY IN ORDINARY TIME

Priest: The Lord's kindness is established for ever.
Filled with gratitude, let us ask our faithful God
to bless us with every good gift.

Minister: That the leaders of the church
will receive the gracious gift of God's wisdom,
let us pray to the Lord:

That the leaders of nations
will receive the gracious gift of God's guidance,
let us pray to the Lord:

That those who suffer from poverty, sickness, and oppression
will receive the gracious gift of God's strengthening,
let us pray to the Lord:

That we will receive the gracious gift of God's hospitality from each other,
let us pray to the Lord:

That those who have died,
especially _____ and _____,
will receive the gracious gift of God's salvation,
let us pray to the Lord:

+

+

Priest: **Gracious God,**
our needs are great,
but your love for us is far greater.
As we walk in the light of your face,
increase in us your many gifts for our
well-being.
Let them become our way to eternal life with
your risen Son,
Jesus Christ, who is Lord for ever and ever.
Amen.

FOURTEENTH SUNDAY IN ORDINARY TIME

Priest: Let us humbly ask our Father, Lord of heaven and earth,
to receive our prayers.

Minister: That the leaders of the church
will accept the yoke of Christ
through lives of gentle and humble service,
let us pray to the Lord:

That the leaders of this and every country
will banish war and promote peace
   throughout the world,
let us pray to the Lord:

That all who are overworked and bear heavy
   responsibilities
may find rest and refreshment,
let us pray to the Lord:

That all who worship here
may trust in Christ and learn discipleship
   through his teaching,
let us pray to the Lord:

That those who have died,
especially _____ and _____,
will celebrate everlasting life in the reign
   of God,
let us pray to the Lord:

+

+

Priest: Most merciful Father,
we ask you to hear the prayers of your church.
Comfort us with your peace,
bless us with your Spirit,
so that our faith and confidence in your Son
may endure all hardships.
We make this prayer through Jesus Christ,
who has revealed you to us.
A just Savior is he, for ever and ever. Amen.

FIFTEENTH SUNDAY IN ORDINARY TIME

Priest: Let us present our petitions to the Lord,
remembering our needs and the needs of
people everywhere.

Minister: For all believers,
that the Word of God give them courage to
correct injustice
and heal the wounds of hate,
let us pray to the Lord:

For young Christians,
that God's Holy Spirit be their
power for witness,
let us pray to the Lord:

For all farmers,
that good weather bring their crops to
maturity
and crown the year with God's bounty,
let us pray to the Lord:

For all who suffer in body, mind, or spirit,
that the sufferings of the present
lead them to the glory promised to us,
let us pray to the Lord:

For those who have died,
especially _____ and _____,
that they rejoice for ever at the heavenly
banquet,
let us pray to the Lord:

For our particular intentions, which we now remember.

[pause for silent prayer]

For all our needs, let us pray to the Lord:

+

+

Priest: Lord God, we ask you to receive our prayers
and answer them according to your great mercy.
Grant that whatever our labors for your kingdom will sow
may produce an abundant harvest for eternity.
We make this prayer through Christ our Lord. Amen.

SIXTEENTH SUNDAY IN ORDINARY TIME

Priest: In the power of the Spirit who helps us to pray rightly,
let us call on our God who cares for us.

Minister: That believers in Jesus Christ will know the Lord's kindness
in living the Gospel,
let us pray to the Lord:

That the human family will know the Lord's kindness
in all that leads to peace and justice,
let us pray to the Lord:

That the poor, the sick, and the persecuted will know the Lord's kindness
in their deliverance from suffering,
let us pray to the Lord:

That we who worship here will know the Lord's kindness in this Eucharist,
let us pray to the Lord:

That those who have died,
especially _____ and _____,
will know the Lord's kindness in everlasting life,
let us pray to the Lord:

+

+

Priest: Wondrous are your deeds, O God, in every
 time and place.
May your will be done in answer to our
 prayers,
so that we may receive your kindness
in what we need this day.
We ask this through Christ our Lord. Amen.

SEVENTEENTH SUNDAY IN ORDINARY TIME

Priest: My sisters and brothers,
let us ask that we will find all things working for our good
in answer to these prayers.

Minister: That the merciful love of God
will come to all who serve the church
and comfort them in difficulty,
let us pray to the Lord:

That the saving wisdom of God
will come to rulers of nations and communities
and shape their thoughts and actions for peace,
let us pray to the Lord:

That the tender compassion of God
will come to those oppressed by any need
and renew their hope in God's promises,
let us pray to the Lord:

That the abundant healing of God
will come to the sick
and raise them up to wholeness of mind and body,
let us pray to the Lord:

That the infinite power of God
will come to us gathered here
and sustain us in the way of God's commands,
let us pray to the Lord:

That the eternal happiness of God
will come to those who have died,
especially _____ and _____,
and be their treasure for ever,
let us pray to the Lord:

+

+

Priest: Gracious God,
as we walk in the light of your face,
increase in us your many gifts for our
    well-being.
Let them become our way to eternal life
with your risen Son, Jesus Christ,
who is Lord for ever and ever. Amen.

EIGHTEENTH SUNDAY IN ORDINARY TIME

Priest: Let us call on the Lord,
who is near to us in every need.

Minister: For those who serve the church,
let us pray to the Lord:

For those who lead nations and communities,
let us pray to the Lord:

For those who suffer from hunger, illness,
and injustice,
let us pray to the Lord:

For those who desire healing of body, mind,
or spirit,
let us pray to the Lord:

For those who are traveling these summer
days,
let us pray to the Lord:

For those who have died in Christ,
especially _____ and _____,
let us pray to the Lord:

✢

✢

Priest: **Lord God,
multiply your blessings among us
as your Son multiplied the loaves and fishes.
Praise and thanksgiving be yours, now and
 always,
through Jesus Christ, our Lord. Amen.**

NINETEENTH SUNDAY IN ORDINARY TIME

Priest: Placing our confidence in God's love,
let us ask for the blessings
that God promises us in the beloved Son.

Minister: That the ministers of the church will reflect
the Lord's kindness
in their service to God's people,
let us pray to the Lord:

That the leaders of nations will find the Lord's
salvation
in their efforts for the good of all,
let us pray to the Lord:

That the poor will know the Lord's justice
in our generous works of charity,
let us pray to the Lord:

That we who assemble here
will recognize the Lord's presence in our
worship,
let us pray to the Lord:

That those who have died,
especially _____ and _____,
will receive the Lord's embrace in everlasting
life,
let us pray to the Lord:

+

+

Priest: **Lord God, your Son leads us on the way of peace.
Draw us to him in this Eucharist,
so that we may rejoice in him now,
and live with him in your presence,
for ever and ever. Amen.**

TWENTIETH SUNDAY IN ORDINARY TIME

Priest: Gathered in this house of prayer,
let us call upon our God.

Minister: That Jews, Christians, and Muslims, and all people of faith
may find renewed strength in God's mercy,
let us pray to the Lord:

That all nations and peoples may find lasting peace
in God's guidance,
let us pray to the Lord:

That the ill, the infirm, and the dying
may find abundant comfort in God's deliverance,
let us pray to the Lord:

That all who worship here
may find welcome joy in God's gifts,
let us pray to the Lord:

That those who have died,
especially _____ and _____,
may find everlasting glory in God's salvation,
let us pray to the Lord:

+

+

Priest: **Lord,
with the persistence of the Canaanite woman
we boldly call out our needs,
for you always listen to the prayers of your
 people.
Grant us your generous blessings in Christ
 Jesus,
both now and for ever. Amen.**

TWENTY-FIRST SUNDAY IN ORDINARY TIME

Priest: The love of the Lord is eternal.
Let us ask the Lord to give us and all people whatever is for our good.

Minister: That the Lord will show great kindness
to the leaders of the church,
and sustain them in their call to service,
let us pray to the Lord:

That the Lord will show great kindness
to the rulers of nations,
and strengthen them in their commitment
 to justice,
let us pray to the Lord:

That the Lord will show great kindness
to the victims of poverty and prejudice,
and answer their cries for help,
let us pray to the Lord:

That the Lord will show great kindness
to those who have died,
especially _____ and _____,
and raise them up to everlasting life,
let us pray to the Lord:

That the Lord will show great kindness to us
as we remember our needs.

[pause for silent prayer]

That the Lord will grant us whatever is
    helpful
and defend us from whatever is harmful,
let us pray to the Lord:

✢

✢

Priest: Lord God, our need for your mercy is great,
but your kindness to us is far greater.
Receive these prayers we have made to you,
and answer them for the sake of your beloved
    Son, Jesus Christ,
who is Lord for ever and ever. Amen.

TWENTY-SECOND SUNDAY IN ORDINARY TIME

Priest: Let us call on the Lord's name
and offer fervent prayer for ourselves and for all people.

Minister: For the ministers of all Christian churches,
that the Lord will uphold them
as they give their lives for the Gospel of Christ,
let us pray to the Lord:

For public officials of this community, state, and nation,
that the Lord will uphold them
as they work to protect our environment,
let us pray to the Lord:

For the poor, the hungry, and the homeless,
that the Lord will uphold them
by our assistance to them,
let us pray to the Lord:

For the sick and the elderly,
that the Lord will uphold them
by our care for them,
let us pray to the Lord:

For all who have died,
especially _____ and _____,
that the Lord will uphold them
in everlasting love,
let us pray to the Lord:

+

+

Priest: Father of our Lord Jesus Christ,
let us see your power and glory
in answer to these prayers.
Make us pleasing in your sight,
so that your will may be done in us and
through us.
We ask this in the name of Jesus, the Lord.
Amen.

TWENTY-THIRD SUNDAY IN ORDINARY TIME

Priest: Let us join our voices and pray for each other's needs
in Jesus' name.

Minister: For the well-being of the holy church of God,
and for the unity of all Christians,
let us pray to the Lord:

For peace in the world, and the reconciliation of states and peoples,
let us pray to the Lord:

For the safety of students and teachers in our schools,
let us pray to the Lord:

For the healing of the sick, the feeding of the hungry,
and the consolation of the afflicted,
let us pray to the Lord:

For the eternal happiness of those who have died,
especially _____ and _____,
let us pray to the Lord:

    +

    +

Priest: God of our salvation,
hear our prayers and watch over us always.
Guide us as your flock, and keep us safe in
    your love.
We ask this through Christ our Lord. Amen.

TWENTY-FOURTH SUNDAY IN ORDINARY TIME

Priest: My brothers and sisters,
with hearts free from anger and hatred
let us humbly bring our petitions before the God of mercy.

Minister: That the Lord's faithful Word will sustain our Holy Father, Pope _____,
the bishops, and all who minister to God's people,
let us pray to the Lord:

That the Lord's guiding hand will direct our public servants
along the paths of justice and peace,
let us pray to the Lord:

That the Lord's mercy for all people will lead nations and families
to share the gift of mutual forgiveness and healing,
let us pray to the Lord:

That the Lord's salvation will speedily deliver the peoples of the world
from poverty, unemployment, starvation and disease,
let us pray to the Lord:

That the Lord's gift of the Eucharist will bind us together
in the new covenant of reconciliation,
let us pray to the Lord:

That the Lord's everlasting love will embrace
the lives of those who have died,
especially _____ and _____,
let us pray to the Lord:

+

+

Priest: God rich in mercy,
grant us what we need to live as your holy
    people.
Let your loving-kindness make us
    compassionate
as you are compassionate,
through Jesus Christ our Lord. Amen.

TWENTY-FIFTH SUNDAY IN ORDINARY TIME

Priest: Let us call on the Lord, who is near to us in every need.

Minister: For catechists and teachers of the Christian faith,
that they proclaim the Lord's greatness
in their service of God's people,
let us pray to the Lord:

For the leaders of governments,
that they reflect the Lord's greatness
in their work for victims of injustice,
let us pray to the Lord:

For those who suffer from sickness,
especially _____ and _____,
that they know the Lord's greatness
in words and deeds of compassion,
let us pray to the Lord:

For us who worship here,
that we imitate the Lord's greatness
in our love for others,
let us pray to the Lord:

For those who have died,
especially _____ and _____,
that they celebrate the Lord's greatness
in the gift of salvation,
let us pray to the Lord:

+

+

Priest: **Gracious God,
give answer to our prayers in your great
 kindness.
Teach us your ways of love,
so that in all we do and say,
we will glorify your holy name.
We ask this through Christ our Lord. Amen.**

TWENTY-SIXTH SUNDAY IN ORDINARY TIME

Priest: Confident that the Lord's kindness is everlasting, let us offer these petitions to the God of mercy.

Minister: That the Lord's goodness will empower the members of the church for generous service, let us pray to the Lord:

That the Lord's guidance will direct our public servants along the paths of justice and peace, let us pray to the Lord:

That the Lord's salvation will speedily deliver the people of this and every country from poverty, starvation, and homelessness, let us pray to the Lord:

That the Lord's compassion will comfort the sick, the aged, and the dying, let us pray to the Lord:

That the Lord's mercy will embrace the lives of those who have died, especially _____ and _____, let us pray to the Lord:

+

+

Priest: God our Savior,
your kindness embraces all peoples,
and your faithfulness knows no limits.
All our hope is in your mercy.
Answer our prayers for the sake of him
whose death shows us the way to life,
your Son, Jesus Christ.
He lives and reigns as Lord, for ever and ever.
　　Amen.

TWENTY-SEVENTH SUNDAY IN ORDINARY TIME

Priest: With loving confidence, we now bring before the Lord
all the needs of the human family.

Minister: That faith may create in the church
a welcome for the prophets of life,
let us pray to the Lord:

That love may create in our society
a welcome for all the unborn,
let us pray to the Lord:

That mercy may create in our world
a welcome for the homeless and the hungry,
let us pray to the Lord:

That compassion may create in our communities
a welcome for the mentally and physically ill,
let us pray to the Lord:

That justice may create around the globe
a welcome for the socially and economically disadvantaged,
let us pray to the Lord:

That divine love may create for those who have died,
especially _____ and _____,
a welcome into everlasting happiness,
let us pray to the Lord:

+

+

Priest: Lord God, Creator and Giver of life,
hear the prayers of your people.
Transform us in your love
so that your kingdom may grow in our midst.
We ask this through Christ our Lord. Amen.

TWENTY-EIGHTH SUNDAY IN ORDINARY TIME

Priest: Let us turn to God in confident prayer,
asking for what we need to live as a holy people.

Minister: That God's goodness will be a source of wisdom
for all the members of the church,
let us pray to the Lord:

That God's goodness will be a source of peace
for nations, peoples, and communities,
let us pray to the Lord:

That God's goodness will be a source of comfort
for those who suffer in mind, body, or spirit,
let us pray to the Lord:

That God's goodness will be a source of holiness for us
as we walk in the way of the Lord,
let us pray to the Lord:

That God's goodness will be a source of everlasting life
for those who have died,
especially _____ and _____,
let us pray to the Lord:

+

+

Priest: God of wisdom and love,
you know our every need even before
we ask.
Show us your goodness in answer to these
prayers,
so that seeking your kingdom may be our joy.
We ask this through Christ our Lord. Amen.

TWENTY-NINTH SUNDAY IN ORDINARY TIME

Priest: Let us present our prayers to the Lord, whose kindness and mercy bring hope to all the earth.

Minister: That missionaries will find renewed strength in God's love,
let us pray to the Lord:

That all nations and peoples
will find lasting peace in God's plan for this world,
let us pray to the Lord:

That the ill,
especially _____ and _____,
will find abundant comfort in God's healing,
let us pray to the Lord:

That all who worship here
will find sure guidance in God's Word,
let us pray to the Lord:

That those who have died,
especially _____ and _____,
will find everlasting joy in God's glory,
let us pray to the Lord:

✢

✢

Priest: **All-holy God,**
we ask you to answer our prayers,
for you are merciful and gracious to all your
     people.
Rescue us from whatever could harm us,
and crown us with your kindness and
     compassion in Christ Jesus,
both now and for ever. Amen.

THIRTIETH SUNDAY IN ORDINARY TIME

Priest: Let us call on our God,
who is compassionate toward us in our need.

Minister: For the welfare of the holy church of God,
and the unity of the human family,
let us pray to the Lord:

For peace throughout the world,
and the reconciliation of states and peoples,
let us pray to the Lord:

For the healing of the sick and the feeding of the hungry,
let us pray to the Lord:

For our deliverance from all affliction and danger,
let us pray to the Lord:

For everlasting light and peace for those who have died,
especially _____ and _____,
let us pray to the Lord:

For our particular needs, which we now remember.

[pause for silent prayer]

For all our needs, let us pray to the Lord:

+

+

Priest: Lord, in your kindness, answer our prayers.
Fill our hearts with the spirit of your charity,
that we may please you in our thoughts and
 actions
and love you in our sisters and brothers.
We ask this through Christ our Lord. Amen.

THIRTY-FIRST SUNDAY IN ORDINARY TIME

Priest: Let us now pray to the one God,
who created all of us.

Minister: That the leaders of the church and of nations
place the desire for service above the desire
for glory,
let us pray to the Lord:

That government officials
will help their people as God's good servants,
let us pray to the Lord:

That those suffering from poverty and
sickness
will be blessed with happiness and hope,
let us pray to the Lord:

That we and our fellow parishioners
will be renewed through the teaching of
Christ,
let us pray to the Lord:

That those who have died,
especially _____ and _____,
will find lasting peace with the Lord,
let us pray to the Lord:

+

+

Priest: **Creating and redeeming God,
we rejoice in your never-failing help.
Show us the greatness of your love,
and answer our prayers in your great mercy.
We ask this through Christ our Lord. Amen.**

THIRTY-SECOND SUNDAY IN ORDINARY TIME

Priest: Let us call upon the Lord,
whose help is near, whose kindness is great.

Minister: For the welfare of the holy churches of God
and for the unity of the human family,
let us pray to the Lord:

For the elimination of disease and famine,
and for peace throughout the world,
let us pray to the Lord:

For wisdom and zeal in the Lord's service,
and for perseverance in doing good,
let us pray to the Lord:

For all that is good and profitable to our salvation,
and for our welcome to the divine wedding feast,
let us pray to the Lord:

For the resurrection of those who have died,
especially _____ and _____,
and for life everlasting with all the saints,
let us pray to the Lord:

✢

✢

Priest: Lord our God,
your mercy is measureless
and your love is beyond words to describe.
Look upon us in your loving-kindness
and grant us the riches of your favor.
We ask this through Christ our Lord. Amen.

THIRTY-THIRD SUNDAY IN ORDINARY TIME

Priest: As children of the day, who face life with hope,
let us pray to God with confidence.

Minister: For the church,
that God may protect and prosper it throughout the world,
let us pray to the Lord:

For civil authorities,
that God may direct them along the ways of all that is good,
let us pray to the Lord:

For those among us who are suffering in mind or body,
that God may deliver them from pain and distress,
let us pray to the Lord:

For this assembly,
that God may empower us to build a more humane world,
let us pray to the Lord:

For those who have gone before us
in the discipleship of Christ,
especially _____ and _____,
that God may grant them refreshment, light, and peace,
let us pray to the Lord:

✚

✚

Priest: Gracious God, giver of all good gifts,
hear our prayers,
so that we may rejoice in the breadth of your
 kindness
and the depth of your mercy.
We ask this through Christ our Lord. Amen.

OUR LORD JESUS CHRIST THE KING

Priest: Let us ask God to hear and answer our prayers,
which we offer in union with Christ our King.

Minister: That God's people will serve Christ the King
by caring for the spiritual and physical needs of his least ones,
let us pray to the Lord:

That leaders of governments will recognize the rights of the oppressed
and honor the dignity of all,
let us pray to the Lord:

That Jesus will come quickly
to save those who wait in suffering, pain, and despair,
let us pray to the Lord:

That we who worship here
will know the goodness and kindness of the Lord at this table,
let us pray to the Lord:

That those who have died,
especially _____ and _____,
will find everlasting joy around God's throne,
let us pray to the Lord:

✛

✛

Priest: Almighty and eternal God,
you willed to restore all things in your
   beloved Son, Jesus Christ.
Help us to live the truth of his kingship
by serving our sisters and brothers with our
   whole heart.
We ask this through Christ our Lord. Amen.

THE MOST HOLY TRINITY

Priest: Having heard the Word of God,
let us now call upon our Father, who made us,
the Son, who redeemed us,
and the Holy Spirit, who renews us,
as we present these petitions.

Minister: That God will guide the Christian churches
in their search for unity,
so that their oneness will show forth
the unity of Father, Son, and Holy Spirit,
let us pray to the Lord:

That God will strengthen civil authorities
in their efforts to establish justice and peace,
let us pray to the Lord:

That God will remove every fear from human hearts
and fill them with that perfect love
which comes from God alone,
let us pray to the Lord:

That God will build up this community for service,
let us pray to the Lord:

That God will help us who have gathered here
to grow in the life of the Holy Trinity
by our celebration of this Eucharist,
let us pray to the Lord:

That God will bring those who have died,
especially _____ and _____,
to share an eternal communion of love,
let us pray to the Lord:

+

+

Priest: Lord God,
have mercy on us and hear our prayers.
Let the love which unites the Persons of the
   Trinity
shape our lives and the lives of all people.
We ask this in the name of Jesus, your Son,
who celebrates life with you and the Holy
   Spirit,
one God, for ever and ever. Amen.

THE MOST HOLY BODY AND BLOOD OF CHRIST

Priest: Let us ask God, our guide and protector,
to be mindful of us in our need.

Minister: That those who lead the churches
will help us live as the one Body of Christ,
let us pray to the Lord:

That national and local government officials
will satisfy the human hunger for peace and
 justice,
let us pray to the Lord:

That those who suffer in body and spirit
will be gladdened by many signs of divine
 and human love for them,
let us pray to the Lord:

That this assembly will delight in Christ's gift
 of himself in the Eucharist,
let us pray to the Lord:

That the dead,
especially _____ and _____,
will be raised up to sing God's praise in
 heaven,
let us pray to the Lord:

+

+

Priest: God our Father,
nothing is lacking to those who love you.
As you fed your people with manna on their
 desert journey,
nourish us on our pilgrim way
with the living Word and the living bread, our
 Lord Jesus Christ.
Hear our prayers for new life in him,
this day and every day,
both now and for ever. Amen.

THE MOST SACRED HEART OF JESUS

Priest: The saving plan of God took flesh in Jesus Christ.
In his most sacred name, let us offer our petitions.

Minister: That God's kindness in the heart of Jesus
will be seen and heard in the mission of the church,
let us pray to the Lord:

That God's peace in the heart of Jesus
will deliver the world from warfare and violence,
let us pray to the Lord:

That God's forgiveness in the heart of Jesus
will bring enemies to forgive each other,
let us pray to the Lord:

That God's compassion in the heart of Jesus
will heal the ills of all who suffer,
let us pray to the Lord:

That God's goodness in the heart of Jesus
will refresh the lives of those who worship here,
let us pray to the Lord:

That God's mercy in the heart of Jesus
will raise up all who have died,
especially _____ and _____,
let us pray to the Lord:

+

+

Priest: **God of the covenant,**
your faithfulness saves us from every danger.
We ask you to answer these prayers
for the sake of your only Son, Jesus Christ,
in whom we find all the treasures of your love,
for ever and ever. Amen.

December 8

THE IMMACULATE CONCEPTION OF THE BLESSED VIRGIN MARY

Priest: The sinless Virgin Mary is God's delight
from all eternity,
and the church's advocate in every age.
As we honor her immaculate conception,
let us join our prayers to hers.

Minister: With holy Mary, mother of Christians,
let us ask unity for the holy church of God
throughout the world.
For this, let us pray to the Lord:

With holy Mary, child of our father Abraham,
let us ask peace for all his descendants
in the Middle East.
For this, let us pray to the Lord:

With holy Mary, helper of the afflicted,
let us ask deliverance from pain and sorrow.
For this, let us pray to the Lord:

With holy Mary, bride of the Holy Spirit,
let us ask the Spirit's power in our lives
these Advent days.
For this, let us pray to the Lord:

With holy Mary, mother of the Son of God,
let us ask eternal life with him
for all who have died,
especially _____ and _____.
For this, let us pray to the Lord:

\+

\+

Priest: God of endless ages,
your Holy Spirit prepared the Blessed Virgin
 Mary
to be a worthy dwelling for your Son.
Through her prayers, offered with ours,
grant what we need to live as her children
and bring us to the glory of your eternal home.
We ask this through Christ our Lord. Amen.

December 12

OUR LADY OF GUADALUPE
(United States of America)

Priest: **In our Lady of Guadalupe,
the desert of our human sorrow
blooms with God's abundant consolation.
As we honor her on this festival day,
let us pray for her children everywhere.**

Minister: **For the welfare of the holy churches of God
and the unity of humankind,
let us pray to the Lord:**

**For the well-being and prosperity
of all the peoples of the Americas,
let us pray to the Lord:**

**For the recovery of the sick,
especially _____ and _____,
and the liberation of the oppressed,
let us pray to the Lord:**

**For our deliverance from hostility
and protection from danger,
let us pray to the Lord:**

**For eternal life and everlasting joy
for those who have died,
especially _____ and _____,
let us pray to the Lord:**

✢

✢

Priest: Lord God,
in the Son of the Blessed Virgin Mary
you have reconciled things earthly and
 heavenly.
Through our prayers,
we commend ourselves, one another,
and our whole life to you,
and ask to stand with Mary in the light of
 your glory,
for ever and ever. Amen.

January (third Monday)

MARTIN LUTHER KING, JR., HOLIDAY
(United States of America)

Priest: **In Dr. Martin Luther King, Jr.,
the truth shines forth:
there is no greater love
than to give one's life for one's friends.
On this day of remembrance,
let us pray for the grace
to love God and neighbor as he did.**

Minister: That Christians receive power
to suffer for the sake of conscience,
let us pray to the Lord:

That public officials receive courage
to oppose injustice and promote equality,
let us pray to the Lord:

That prophets in our midst receive strength
to glory in the cross of persecution,
let us pray to the Lord:

That we receive deliverance
from all sin and from fear of death,
let us pray to the Lord:

That those who have died,
especially _____ and _____,
receive everlasting life with Jesus Christ,
the faithful witness,
let us pray to the Lord:

+

+

Priest: **God of martyrs,
hear our prayers as we give thanks
for the ministry of Dr. Martin Luther King, Jr.,
so that his dream may give us hope
and transform our world for your glory,
both now and for ever. Amen.**

March 19

ST. JOSEPH, HUSBAND OF THE BLESSED VIRGIN MARY

Priest: With faith in God's promises,
let us present our needs and petitions in company with Saint Joseph.

Minister: That God's compassion will endure
as the heart of the church's ministry,
let us pray to the Lord:

That God's peace will endure
as the unity of nations and peoples,
let us pray to the Lord:

That God's salvation will endure
as healing for the sick and injured,
especially _____ and _____,
let us pray to the Lord:

That God's faithfulness will endure
as our hope in God's goodness,
let us pray to the Lord:

That God's kindness will endure
as eternal life for those who have died,
especially _____ and _____,
let us pray to the Lord:

          +

          +

Priest: **Blessed is Saint Joseph, O Lord,
and all who dwell in your house.
Receive our prayers for the saving love
you have revealed in our Savior, Jesus
    Christ,
who lives and reigns for ever and ever. Amen.**

March 25

THE ANNUNCIATION OF THE LORD

Priest: Coming among us to do God's will,
Jesus Christ destroyed our death
and made us alive for God.
Let us offer our petitions to the God who saves.

Minister: That God will be with the members of the church
in their words and deeds,
let us pray to the Lord:

That God will be with government officials
in their planning and decisions,
let us pray to the Lord:

That God will be with those who suffer
in their deliverance from poverty, illness, and prejudice,
let us pray to the Lord:

That God will be with us
in the Word made flesh for our salvation,
let us pray to the Lord:

That God will be with those who have died,
especially _____ and _____,
in the assembly of God's holy ones,
let us pray to the Lord:

✢

✢

Priest: **Lord God,
your Son, Jesus Christ, was born of the Virgin Mary
to consecrate us in your truth.
Unite our prayers to hers,
and make us, like her,
hearers of your Word and doers of your will.
We ask this through the same Christ our Lord.
Amen.**

MEMORIAL DAY
(United States of America)

Priest: Let us confidently pray to the God of mercy,
who raised the beloved Son from death
as the firstfruits of eternal life.

Minister: For the salvation of all who follow the Gospel
of Christ,
let us pray to the Lord:

For the reign of God in this world,
let us pray to the Lord:

For the safety of travelers this holiday
weekend,
let us pray to the Lord:

For a place of refreshment, light, and peace
for all who have died,
especially defenders of our country,
let us pray to the Lord:

For the final destruction of sin and the grave
by the power of the risen Christ,
let us pray to the Lord:

✛

✛

Priest: God of the dead and the living,
in your kindness grant what we have asked
   of you,
for we commend ourselves, one another,
and all the faithful departed to your Son,
   Jesus Christ,
who is Lord for ever and ever. Amen.

June 24

THE NATIVITY OF ST. JOHN THE BAPTIST

Priest: Let us pray to our God,
asking that the example of John the Baptist
may shape our lives.

Minister: That like John the Baptist,
we may know how to advance Christ's work
in the world,
let us pray to the Lord:

That like John,
we may direct all our actions to the service of
Christ,
let us pray to the Lord:

That like John,
we may bear with courage
every suffering that witness to Christ brings us,
let us pray to the Lord:

That like John,
we may rejoice in the reign of God
made incarnate in Jesus Christ,
let us pray to the Lord:

That like John,
those who have died,
especially _____ and _____,
may enjoy the peace promised to those
who seek Christ in all things,
let us pray to the Lord:

+

+

Priest: Lord God, in the fullness of time
you revealed yourself to John the Baptist
in the coming of your Son.
Through these prayers,
help us to be always ready
to welcome Jesus Christ here in our midst
and in our sisters and brothers.
We ask this through the same Christ our Lord.
   Amen.

June 29

SAINT PETER AND SAINT PAUL, APOSTLES

Priest: With the holy apostles Peter and Paul,
let us bring our needs and the needs of all
   people to the Lord.

Minister: For the strength of the Catholic faith
that comes to us from the apostles,
let us pray to the Lord:

    For God's blessing on people, parishes, and
       communities
    that bear the name of Saints Peter and Paul,
    let us pray to the Lord:

    For the safety and success
    of the missionary apostolate of the church,
    even to the ends of the earth,
    let us pray to the Lord:

    For the preaching of the Gospel by word and
       deed,
    let us pray to the Lord:

    For the everlasting joy of those who have
       died,
    especially _____ and _____,
    let us pray to the Lord:

Let us ask the Lord to help, save, and defend us
as we remember our needs.

[pause for silent prayer]

For the needs we hold in our hearts,
let us pray to the Lord:

+

+

Priest: Heavenly Father,
your risen Son commissioned his chosen apostles
to preach the good news to all creation.
By the prayers of Saints Peter and Paul,
strengthen us with apostolic teaching
and empower us to be your faithful witnesses
in the world.
We ask this through Christ our Lord. Amen.

July 4

INDEPENDENCE DAY
(United States of America)

Priest: From God alone comes our salvation.
On this Independence Day,
let us pour out our hearts before the Lord in fervent prayer.

Minister: For the unity of the church in the United States,
and for a life-giving share in the gifts of God,
let us pray to the Lord:

For peace throughout the whole world,
and for the prosperity of the human family,
let us pray to the Lord:

For the safety of those who serve in the armed forces,
and the well-being of their families,
let us pray to the Lord:

For an end to every threat to human life,
and for the elimination of hunger and disease,
let us pray to the Lord:

For the recovery of the sick and the relief of the poor,
let us pray to the Lord:

For the blessings of good weather throughout these summer days,
and for bountiful crops,
let us pray to the Lord:

For the consolation of the dying,
and eternal life for those who have died,
especially _____ and _____,
let us pray to the Lord:

+

+

Priest: Rock of our strength,
you never forsake your people,
but remember them in your great love.
We place our trust in you,
and ask your generous blessings in Christ
    Jesus,
both now and for ever. Amen.

August 15

THE ASSUMPTION OF THE BLESSED VIRGIN MARY

Priest: Let us ask God to receive our petitions
in the throne room of heaven,
where the glorious Virgin Mary powerfully
prays for us.

Minister: For servants of the church,
called to minister God's salvation,
let us pray to the Lord:

For public officials,
called to promote God's justice and peace,
let us pray to the Lord:

For the lowly of the earth,
called to share a place of honor with Jesus
Christ,
let us pray to the Lord:

For us gathered here,
called to welcome Christ the Lord in this
Eucharist,
let us pray to the Lord:

For those who have died,
called to receive the mercy of God,
especially _____ and _____,
let us pray to the Lord:

✢

✢

Priest: **God of Elizabeth and Mary,**
great were your saving deeds in their lives;
great is your merciful care in ours.
Come to our help in answer to these prayers,
for we offer them in the name of Jesus Christ,
your Anointed One,
who is Lord for ever and ever. Amen.

September (first Monday)

LABOR DAY
(United States of America and Canada)

Priest: As we give thanks for the work that sustains our lives
and fulfills God's plan for our world,
let us offer these petitions to the God of mercy.

Minister: For the church,
that it extend God's saving work to all nations,
let us pray to the Lord:

For workers in this and every land,
that they enjoy respect, safety,
and just compensation for their labor,
let us pray to the Lord:

For those who cannot find jobs or keep them,
that they receive assistance in their need,
let us pray to the Lord:

For us who worship here,
that we accomplish God's redemptive purpose
in the many places of our work,
let us pray to the Lord:

For those who have died,
especially _____ and _____,
that they enjoy eternal rest with God,
let us pray to the Lord:

+

+

Priest: **Lord God,
we ask you to answer these prayers,
so that we can bring the fullness of our
 intelligence,
strength, and care to our work
and glorify you in all things.
We ask this through Jesus Christ, the Lord.
 Amen.**

September 14

THE EXALTATION OF THE HOLY CROSS

Priest: The Lord Jesus humbled himself
and became obedient unto death,
even to death on a cross.
In the power of his resurrection from the dead,
let us pray that all people will be raised up
to new life in Christ the Lord.

Minister: Christ crucified became like us in our weakness;
through his Cross,
may the church become like him in his saving power.
For this, let us pray to the Lord:

Christ crucified became like the poor and the oppressed in their need;
through his Cross,
may they become like him in his triumph over injustice.
For this, let us pray to the Lord:

Christ crucified became like us in our sorrows;
through his Cross,
may all who suffer become like him in his lasting joy.
For this, let us pray to the Lord:

Christ crucified became like us in our human
   lowliness;
through his Cross,
may we become like him in his divine glory.
For this, let us pray to the Lord:

Christ crucified became like the dead in their
   emptiness;
through his Cross,
may those who have died,
especially _____ and _____,
become like him in his fullness of life.
For this, let us pray to the Lord:

+

+

Priest: Lord God,
answer our prayers in your great mercy,
so that the mystery of our redemption in the
   Cross of Christ
may transform us and the world you love.
We ask this through our crucified yet risen
   Savior,
Jesus Christ, who is Lord for ever and ever.
   Amen.

November 1

ALL SAINTS

Priest: Gathered in the holy presence of God,
let us pray for our world and for all who dwell in it.

Minister: That the church will receive God's blessing
in its desire for holiness,
let us pray to the Lord:

That all nations will receive God's blessing
in freedom from injustice and war,
let us pray to the Lord:

That those who serve in public office will
receive God's blessing
in promoting the common good,
let us pray to the Lord:

That those who suffer from poverty, illness,
and homelessness
will receive God's blessing in renewed hope,
let us pray to the Lord:

That this assembly of God's children will
receive God's blessing
in this sacrifice of thanksgiving,
let us pray to the Lord:

That those who have died,
especially _____ and _____,
will receive God's blessing in everlasting
glory,
let us pray to the Lord:

+

+

Priest: With all the saints around your throne, O God,
we offer prayers that reach toward praise.
Let us rejoice and be glad in your love
as we celebrate life in the kingdom of your
    Son, Jesus Christ,
who is Lord for ever and ever. Amen.

November 2

COMMEMORATION OF ALL THE FAITHFUL DEPARTED
(All Souls)

Priest: Blessed is the Lord our God,
Ruler of life and death,
for raising the beloved Son as the firstborn
    from the dead.
In his life-giving name,
let us pray that all who sleep in Christ
will awake to share his glory.

Minister: The Lord Jesus raised the widow's son to life.
In his name, let us ask God's unending life
for our deceased relatives and friends.
For this, let us pray to the Lord:

The Lord Jesus wept for Lazarus
when he lay in the tomb.
In his name, let us ask God's consolation
for all who mourn.
For this, let us pray to the Lord:

The Lord Jesus promised paradise
to the repentant thief.
In his name, let us ask God's happiness
for all who died in great misery and suffering.
For this, let us pray to the Lord:

The Lord Jesus fed the hungry and healed the sick.
In his name, let us ask God's refreshment
for victims of war, neglect, starvation, and disease.
For this, let us pray to the Lord:

The Lord Jesus redeemed his faithful ones through the Cross.
In his name, let us ask God's salvation
for our fellow parishioners who have died,
especially _____ and _____,
and for all God's servants.
For this, let us pray to the Lord:

+

+

Priest: Holy, immortal God,
you are the source of everlasting life for all your people.
Grant forgiveness and peace
to those whom we remember today at your altar.
We ask this in the name of Jesus the Lord.
Amen.

November 9

THE DEDICATION OF THE LATERAN BASILICA IN ROME

Priest: We are God's building,
the living stones rising on a firm foundation in Christ Jesus.
In the power of the Holy Spirit who dwells within us,
let us offer fervent prayers to the Lord.

Minister: That the church will gather into one
the scattered children of God throughout the world,
let us pray to the Lord:

That believers of all religions
will be able to worship God in freedom and peace,
let us pray to the Lord:

That architects, designers, and artists will use their talents
to reveal the glory of God,
let us pray to the Lord:

That we who render devoted service to God in this Eucharist
will render generous help to our needy brothers and sisters,
let us pray to the Lord:

That all who have died,
especially _____ and _____,
will find a dwelling place in God's eternal
    home,
let us pray to the Lord:

+

+

Priest: Lord God, wise builder of your church,
we ask you to answer the prayers
we have offered in your holy house.
Raise us to share the everlasting glory of your
    risen Son,
Jesus Christ, who is Lord for ever and ever.
    Amen.

THANKSGIVING DAY
(United States of America)

Priest: God has cared for our nation from its beginning,
but God has always invited us to pray.
On this day of grateful celebration,
let us offer our petitions.

Minister: For those who are called to ministry in the church,
that they work for its unity and peace,
let us pray to the Lord:

For those who serve in public office,
that they lead us with love for justice,
let us pray to the Lord:

For all who produce food for the world,
that they receive a just return for their labor,
let us pray to the Lord:

For all who work for the well-being of the human family,
that they rejoice in the hope they give to others,
let us pray to the Lord:

For the sick of our community,
especially _____ and _____,
that we surround them with our love and compassion,
let us pray to the Lord:

For ourselves and those dear to us,
that we find strength in our mutual love,
let us pray to the Lord:

For those who have died,
especially _____ and _____,
that they sing the everlasting song of
    thanksgiving in heaven,
let us pray to the Lord:

+

+

Priest: Generous God,
in these prayers we open our hands
to receive your abundant gifts,
and we open our hearts to share them with
    others.
Bless our receiving and our giving,
we humbly ask,
for we call out in the name of Jesus,
who is Lord for ever and ever. Amen.

Year B

FIRST SUNDAY OF ADVENT

Priest: Let us lift up our prayers to God our Father,
who faithfully shapes our lives
for the coming of the beloved Son.

Minister: That the church will know the Lord's favor
in watchful readiness for the revelation of Christ,
let us pray to the Lord:

That leaders of governments will know the Lord's favor
in fervent efforts to end injustice, poverty, and war,
let us pray to the Lord:

That the sick and hospitalized will know the Lord's favor
in abundant health and strength,
let us pray to the Lord:

That this assembly will know the Lord's favor
in untiring service until the Master returns,
let us pray to the Lord:

That those who have died,
especially _____ and _____,
will know the Lord's favor in everlasting joy,
let us pray to the Lord:

    +

    +

Priest: God our redeemer, mercifully hear our prayers.
Make us mindful of your ways once more.
Renew in our lives your wonders of old,
so that the appointed time of Christ's coming
will find us blameless in your sight.
We ask this through Christ our Lord. Amen.

SECOND SUNDAY OF ADVENT

Priest: Let us pray that all people will see the Lord's salvation
in answer to these prayers.

Minister: That the glory of the Lord will be revealed
in the church's search for holiness,
let us pray to the Lord:

That the glory of the Lord will be revealed
in works of justice and peace throughout the world,
let us pray to the Lord:

That the glory of the Lord will be revealed
in comfort for the sick and injured,
especially _____ and _____,
let us pray to the Lord:

That the glory of the Lord will be revealed
in our preparation for the day of God,
let us pray to the Lord:

That the glory of the Lord will be revealed
in eternal happiness for those who have died,
especially _____ and _____,
let us pray to the Lord:

+

+

Priest: God our shepherd, come into our lives
with your power to help, save, and defend us,
and let us see your loving-kindness in your
   Son,
Jesus Christ, both now and for ever. Amen.

THIRD SUNDAY OF ADVENT

Priest: "Pray without ceasing," says Saint Paul.
So let us ask God to do great things for us and
   for our world
as we offer these prayers.

Minister: That God will make holiness spring up
in all the members of the church,
let us pray to the Lord:

That God will make love for justice and peace
   spring up
in our public servants,
let us pray to the Lord:

That God will make care for the environment
   spring up
in human hearts,
let us pray to the Lord:

That God will make thankful praise spring up
in us who prepare for the celebration of
   Christmas,
let us pray to the Lord:

That God will make eternal happiness spring
   up
in those who have died,
especially _____ and _____,
let us pray to the Lord:

+

+

Priest: Ever-faithful God,
remember your promise of mercy
as we offer these petitions.
Accomplish your saving plan for us
and make us, like John the Baptist,
eager to embrace your will for our world in
   Jesus Christ,
who is Lord for ever and ever. Amen.

FOURTH SUNDAY OF ADVENT

Priest: My brothers and sisters,
we know that all things are possible with God,
and so we confidently ask the Lord to hear our prayers.

Minister: The Father made Mary to be highly favored.
Let us ask that the church will share in Mary's holiness and humility.
For this, let us pray to the Lord:

The Father promised that Mary's Son would have great dignity.
Let us ask that the leaders of nations
will promote the human dignity of their people.
For this, let us pray to the Lord:

The Father revealed to Mary in many ways
that God was close to her.
Let us ask that people in every need,
especially travelers,
will know the saving presence of God.
For this, let us pray to the Lord:

The Father made Mary the most blessed of women.
Let us ask the blessings of her faith and obedience
for this assembly.
For this, let us pray to the Lord:

The Father promised Mary that her Son
  would sit upon the throne of David.
Let us ask that those who have died,
especially _____ and _____,
will rejoice around his throne for ever.
For this, let us pray to the Lord:

+

+

Priest: Father most holy,
we ask you to answer these prayers,
for we pray only that your will be done in us.
To you who alone are wise,
may glory be given through your Son, Jesus,
both now and for ever. Amen.

December 24

CHRISTMAS EVE

Priest: Rejoicing in God's abundant kindness and generous love
made incarnate in Jesus Christ,
let us ask these blessings for the church and for the world.

Minister: That God's favor will rest on the ministers of the church
as they serve God's people,
let us pray to the Lord:

That God's favor will rest on all nations and peoples
as they seek to live in harmony,
let us pray to the Lord:

That God's favor will rest on all who suffer in body, mind, or spirit
as they welcome the salvation of God,
let us pray to the Lord:

That God's favor will rest on us
as we seek to live as God's own people,
let us pray to the Lord:

That God's favor will rest on those who have died,
especially _____ and _____,
as they live for ever in God's kingdom of peace,
let us pray to the Lord:

✢

✢

Priest: God of our salvation, we rejoice this night
in the birth of your beloved Son, Jesus Christ.
Let your favor prepare us to welcome his
 appearing in glory,
so that we may sing your praise in his
 presence,
for ever and ever. Amen.

December 25

CHRISTMAS DAY

Priest: Let us present our needs to almighty God
through Jesus Christ,
the heir of all things for our salvation.

Minister: That the love of God in Jesus Christ
will empower the church's mission to the
nations,
let us pray to the Lord:

That the peace of God in Jesus Christ
will reconcile the peoples of the world,
especially in the land of his birth,
let us pray to the Lord:

That the compassion of God in Jesus Christ
will heal the sick and comfort the sorrowful,
let us pray to the Lord:

That the grace of God in Jesus Christ
will gladden this assembly of God's people,
let us pray to the Lord:

That the mercy of God in Jesus Christ
will bring those who have died,
especially _____ and _____,
into the glory of heaven,
let us pray to the Lord:

✢

✢

Priest: **God our Savior,
on this holy day, in this holy house,
we receive the fullness of your love in Jesus
    Christ.
Help us to share that love generously
with our sisters and brothers,
so that all may give thanks to your holy name,
both now and for ever. Amen.**

THE HOLY FAMILY OF JESUS, MARY, AND JOSEPH

Priest: Let us seek the Lord's gifts for the family of God
in these prayers.

Minister: That pastors and teachers will receive strength
from our ever-faithful God,
let us pray to the Lord:

That heads of governments will receive wisdom
from our ever-wise God,
let us pray to the Lord:

That families will receive the gift of mutual love
from our ever-caring God,
let us pray to the Lord:

That those who are sick or injured will receive healing
from our ever-providing God,
let us pray to the Lord:

That this assembly will receive whatever is helpful
from our ever-watchful God,
let us pray to the Lord:

That those who have gone to God in peace,
especially _____ and _____,
will receive the joy of the resurrection
from our ever-living God,
let us pray to the Lord:

✛

✛

Priest: Lord God, with Abraham and Sarah,
we trust in your promise of blessing;
with Anna and Simeon, we welcome your
 blessing made incarnate
in Jesus Christ, the bringer of your new
 covenant with us.
Let your favor rest on us, his sisters and
 brothers,
in answer to these prayers,
so that we may rejoice in your goodness,
both now and for ever. Amen.

January 1

THE BLESSED VIRGIN MARY, THE MOTHER OF GOD

Priest: In company with the great Mother of God, Mary most-holy, let us ask to know God's gracious care in these petitions.

Minister: That God's faithfulness in Jesus Christ will support those who serve God's people, let us pray to the Lord:

That God's peace in Jesus Christ will guide leaders of this and every land, let us pray to the Lord:

That God's salvation in Jesus Christ will deliver those who are sick, hungry, and homeless, let us pray to the Lord:

That God's love in Jesus Christ will bless and keep us during this new year, let us pray to the Lord:

That God's mercy in Jesus Christ will raise up those who have died, especially _____ and _____, let us pray to the Lord:

✢

✢

Priest: **Abba, Father,**
we rejoice in what we have heard and seen
in your beloved Son born of Mary, Jesus Christ.
In his most sacred name,
we ask to receive your abundant gifts,
this day and every day, both now and for ever.
Amen.

SECOND SUNDAY AFTER CHRISTMAS
(where Epiphany is observed on January 6)

Priest: As we give thanks for God's blessings,
let us offer our prayers for each other and for all in need.

Minister: That God's grace in Christ the Shepherd
will guide our Pope, our (arch) bishop, our pastor,
and all who serve our parish,
let us pray to the Lord:

That God's grace in Christ the peacemaker
will uphold world leaders and local officials
in their work for peace,
let us pray to the Lord:

That God's grace in Christ the liberator
will deliver those who are ill, hungry, or homeless,
let us pray to the Lord:

That God's grace in Christ the Savior
will enlighten us who worship here,
let us pray to the Lord:

That God's grace in Christ the life-giver
will raise those who have died,
especially _____ and _____,
to eternal joy,
let us pray to the Lord:

+

+

Priest: **Father,
grant us the riches of your grace
in answer to these prayers,
so that we will rejoice in your Son, Jesus
    Christ,
who dwells with us, both now and for ever.
    Amen.**

THE EPIPHANY OF THE LORD

Priest: Let us call upon the God
whose everlasting love rescues the poor and the afflicted.

Minister: That the power of Christ will be light
for those who face the darkness of religious persecution,
let us pray to the Lord:

That the peace of Christ will be light
for those who struggle in the darkness of war, especially refugees,
let us pray to the Lord:

That the compassion of Christ will be light
for those who suffer the darkness of famine, disease, poverty, and homelessness,
let us pray to the Lord:

That the courage of Christ will be light
for all who live in the darkness of fear,
let us pray to the Lord:

That the mercy of Christ will be light
for all who have known the darkness of death,
especially _____ and _____,
let us pray to the Lord:

    +

    +

Priest: God of all the earth,
as we joyfully proclaim your praises with the
    magi,
we ask your salvation in Jesus Christ
for ourselves and for all in need.
He is Lord for ever and ever. Amen.

THE BAPTISM OF THE LORD

Priest: In the most sacred name of Jesus,
who was anointed priest, prophet, and king at his baptism,
let us pray for our needs and the needs of all people.

Minister: For all those who believe in Christ the Lord
through baptism in water and the Holy Spirit,
let us pray to the Lord:

For those who are preparing for Christian initiation
in our parish and in our (arch)diocese,
let us pray to the Lord:

For those who are crushed by military conflicts and civil strife throughout the world,
let us pray to the Lord:

For those who suffer from mental or physical illness
and for those who care for them,
let us pray to the Lord:

For us who listen to God's beloved Son
in his holy Word
and receive him in his holy sacrament,
let us pray to the Lord:

> For those who have died believing that Jesus
>   is the Christ, their Savior,
> especially _____ and _____,
> let us pray to the Lord:
>
> +
>
> +

Priest: Lord God,
> let us draw water joyfully from the springs of
>   your mercy
> in answer to these prayers.
> Renew within us the abundant power for
>   good
> that is your baptismal gift to us
> and to all who place their hope in your Son,
>   Jesus Christ,
> who is Lord for ever and ever. Amen.

ASH WEDNESDAY

Priest: Let us ask the God of mercy to help, save and defend us
in answer to these prayers.

Minister: For a deeper commitment to pray, fast, and help the needy
as the Lord wills,
let us pray to the Lord:

For the grace of the Holy Spirit
in the hearts of those preparing for Christian initiation at Easter,
let us pray to the Lord:

For an end to injustice, poverty, and warfare
through all the earth,
let us pray to the Lord:

For our deliverance from sin, sickness, and affliction,
let us pray to the Lord:

For the eternal happiness of those who have died,
especially _____ and _____,
let us pray to the Lord:

+

+

Priest: God rich in kindness,
we ask you to answer these prayers,
so that our Lenten observance
may draw us closer to you in holiness
and closer to each other in repentance.
We ask this through Christ our Lord. Amen.

FIRST SUNDAY OF LENT

Priest: Let us call upon the God
who has made a lasting covenant with us in
Jesus Christ.

Minister: That the Lord will remember the leaders of
the church
and guide them in the way of service,
let us pray to the Lord:

That the Lord will remember those chosen
today
for Christian initiation at Easter,
especially _____ and _____,
and guide them in the way of faith,
let us pray to the Lord:

That the Lord will remember the rulers of
nations and communities
and guide them in the way of justice and
peace,
let us pray to the Lord:

That the Lord will remember those who suffer
in body, mind, or spirit,
and guide them in the way of salvation,
let us pray to the Lord:

That the Lord will remember us who worship
here,
and guide us in the way of repentance,
let us pray to the Lord:

That the Lord will remember those who have died,
especially _____ and _____,
and guide them in the way of eternal life,
let us pray to the Lord:

+

+

Priest: Lord God, as we remember your beloved Son, Jesus Christ, in this Eucharist,
we ask you to remember us, his sisters and brothers,
and strengthen us to follow your ways of love and truth.
We make this prayer through the same Christ our Lord. Amen.

SECOND SUNDAY OF LENT

Priest: My sisters and brothers,
let us place before the God of salvation
our own needs and the needs of all people.

Minister: For the elect of the church,
especially _____ and _____,
that they be ready to embrace new life in the
 waters of baptism,
let us pray to the Lord:

For the leaders of nations and governments,
that they achieve peace and justice for their
 people,
let us pray to the Lord:

For all who stand firm in the face of tyranny
 and oppression,
that they find strength in the saving power of
 Jesus Christ,
let us pray to the Lord:

For all who lack food, shelter, or employment,
for all who are lonely, sick, or injured,
that they receive God's assistance at our
 hands,
let us pray to the Lord:

For us, God's holy people assembled here,
that we celebrate the paschal feast
in the freedom of God's children,
let us pray to the Lord:

For those who have died,
especially _____ and _____,
that they rejoice in their deliverance from
    death,
let us pray to the Lord:

+

+

Priest: Lord God, source of love and giver of
    blessings,
we confidently ask you to give us those things
that will strengthen us as your servants these
    Lenten days,
through Jesus Christ, our Lord. Amen.

THIRD SUNDAY OF LENT

Priest: Gathered in this house of prayer, let us call upon our God.

Minister: That all the members of the church
and those preparing to become members,
especially _____ and _____,
may find renewed strength in God's mercy,
let us pray to the Lord:

That all nations and peoples may find lasting peace
in God's plan for this world,
let us pray to the Lord:

That the ill, infirm, and the dying
may find abundant comfort in God's love,
let us pray to the Lord:

That all who worship here
may find sure guidance in God's wisdom,
let us pray to the Lord:

That those who have died,
especially _____ and _____,
may find everlasting joy in the temple of God's glory,
let us pray to the Lord:

+

+

Priest: **Lord,
you faithfully listen to the prayers of your
   people
in every time and place.
We put our trust in you,
and ask your generous blessings in Christ
   Jesus,
both now and for ever. Amen.**

FOURTH SUNDAY OF LENT

Priest: Great and everlasting is God's love for us.
Let us earnestly ask the Father to show us the
  wealth of divine love
as we present our needs.

Minister: For the unity of all who believe in the name of
  God's only Son,
and for the faith of those preparing for
  membership in the church,
especially _____ and _____,
let us pray to the Lord:

For peace throughout the whole world,
and for the well-being of the human family,
let us pray to the Lord:

For an end to every threat against human life,
and for the elimination of hunger and disease,
let us pray to the Lord:

For the recovery of the sick and the relief of
  the poor,
let us pray to the Lord:

For the consolation of the dying,
and eternal life for those who have died,
especially _____ and _____,
let us pray to the Lord:

+

+

Priest: God rich in mercy,
we ask you to answer us in our need,
and fill us with your saving grace.
Let our prayers be a source of new life for us
and for the world you love.
We ask this through Jesus Christ,
the one in whom we find your kindness,
both now and for ever. Amen.

FIFTH SUNDAY OF LENT

Priest: In company with Christ, the source of our salvation,
let us offer our fervent prayers to the God of mercy.

Minister: That the ministers of the church will know the Lord
in their generous self-sacrifice,
let us pray to the Lord:

That those who are preparing for baptism
[and for reception into the Catholic Church],
especially _____ and _____,
will know the Lord in their obedient faith,
let us pray to the Lord:

That the citizens of this and every land will know the Lord
in their untiring pursuit of justice and peace,
let us pray to the Lord:

That we will know the Lord
in our Lenten prayer, fasting, and service,
let us pray to the Lord:

That those who have died,
especially _____ and _____,
will know the Lord in the divine gift of eternal life,
let us pray to the Lord:

+

+

Priest: **Lord God,**
we ask you to receive our prayers
and answer them according to your great mercy.
Grant that our death and burial with Christ in baptism
may produce an abundant harvest for eternity.
We ask this through the same Christ our Lord.
Amen.

PALM SUNDAY OF THE LORD'S PASSION

Priest: The Lord Jesus emptied himself of divine privilege
and accepted death on a cross for our salvation.
In his most sacred name, let us offer our petitions.

Minister: For those preparing to receive the paschal sacraments at Easter,
especially _____ and _____,
let us pray to the Lord:

For liturgical ministers who will assist us
in celebrating the Lord's passover this Holy Week,
let us pray to the Lord:

For those who serve the needs of the sick and the poor,
here in our parish and far away,
let us pray to the Lord:

For those who await the healing power and mercy of Jesus, God's Suffering Servant,
especially _____ and _____,
let us pray to the Lord:

For those who have died in company with their crucified Lord,
especially _____ and _____,
let us pray to the Lord:

✢

✢

Priest: **Lord God,
as we enter this week of grace with your
   beloved Son,
be our help in every need.
May our worship in this holy house
and our service to others outside it
proclaim that "Jesus Christ is Lord."
In this be your glory, both now and for ever.
   Amen.**

HOLY THURSDAY

Priest: On this night of remembrance and thanksgiving
let us call upon the name of the Lord in these prayers.

Minister: That the new passover made by the Lord Jesus
will be the strength of Pope _____,
_____, our (arch)bishop,
the clergy, and all who minister to God's people,
let us pray to the Lord:

That the reconciliation accomplished by the Lord Jesus
will be the goal of civil authorities in every land,
let us pray to the Lord:

That the banquet prepared by the Lord Jesus
will be the consolation of those who suffer in body, mind, and spirit,
let us pray to the Lord:

That the new covenant sealed by the Lord Jesus
will be the salvation of us who worship here,
let us pray to the Lord:

That the everlasting life won by the Lord Jesus
will be the happiness of those who have died,
especially _____ and _____,
let us pray to the Lord:

+

+

Priest: Nourishing God,
as we prepare to receive the Body of Christ
broken for us
and his Blood poured out for us,
help us to give his saving love generously to
others.
We ask this through the same Christ our Lord.
Amen.

HOLY SATURDAY: EASTER VIGIL

Priest: In the joy of Christ's holy and life-giving resurrection, let us offer our petitions.

Minister: That God's glorious triumph in the risen Christ
will renew the members of the church,
let us pray to the Lord:

That God's glorious triumph in the risen Christ
will gladden those newly initiated
[and received into the Church] this night,
especially _____ and _____,
let us pray to the Lord:

That God's glorious triumph in the risen Christ
will establish all nations and peoples in peace,
let us pray to the Lord:

That God's glorious triumph in the risen Christ
will deliver the sick and injured from their distress,
let us pray to the Lord:

That God's glorious triumph in the risen Christ
will enliven us who worship here,
let us pray to the Lord:

That God's glorious triumph in the risen
    Christ
will raise those who have died,
especially _____ and _____,
to everlasting happiness,
let us pray to the Lord:

✢

✢

Priest: **Creating and redeeming God,
your mercy endures for ever in the risen
    Christ.
Let us and all your people share that mercy,
this most holy night, and for ever and ever.
    Amen.**

EASTER SUNDAY: THE RESURRECTION OF THE LORD

Priest: On this day made glorious above all others
by the resurrection of Jesus Christ,
let us pray for our needs and the needs of
people everywhere.

Minister: That all the members of the church,
especially those newly initiated,
[and received into the church,]
_____ and _____,
will rejoice in God's surpassing power for
good
in the risen Christ,
let us pray to the Lord:

That leaders of nations and communities
will rejoice in God's lasting peace in the risen
Christ,
let us pray to the Lord:

That the sick, especially _____ and
_____,
will rejoice in God's abundant healing in the
risen Christ,
let us pray to the Lord:

That we who celebrate the paschal feast
will rejoice in God's loving-kindness in the
risen Christ,
let us pray to the Lord:

That those who have died,
especially _____ and _____,
will rejoice in God's eternal salvation in the
    risen Christ,
let us pray to the Lord:

✦

✦

Priest: **God of glory,**
wonderful are your works in your Son, Jesus
    Christ,
whom you have made the cornerstone of our
    lives.
Grant us what we need
to live as the people who rejoice in him,
this day and every day,
both now and for ever. Amen.

SECOND SUNDAY OF EASTER
(Divine Mercy Sunday)

Priest: All of God's infinite goodness is ours in Jesus Christ, now and always.
Let us pray to know God's everlasting love in the risen Lord.

Minister: That all Christians, especially those initiated [and received into the Church] at Easter,
_____ and _____,
find abundant life in Jesus Christ, the Son of God,
let us pray to the Lord:

That the peoples of the earth
find abundant life in Jesus Christ, the peace of God,
let us pray to the Lord:

That those who are weakened by illness and injury,
especially _____ and _____,
find abundant life in Jesus Christ, the healing of God,
let us pray to the Lord:

That all oppressed by fear and sorrow
find abundant life in Jesus Christ, the compassion of God,
let us pray to the Lord:

That our community find abundant life in
 Jesus Christ, the strength of God,
let us pray to the Lord:

That those who have died,
especially _____ and _____,
find abundant and everlasting life in Jesus
 Christ, the mercy of God,
let us pray to the Lord:

+

+

Priest: Your mercy endures for ever, O God,
and extends wider than our needs.
Receive these prayers and answer them
for the sake of Jesus, your beloved Son,
whose triumph over death is wonderful in our
 eyes,
both now and for ever. Amen.

THIRD SUNDAY OF EASTER

Priest: In grateful confidence,
let us ask the Father to hear our petitions,
so that the love of God may come to perfection in us.

Minister: That the church will powerfully proclaim to all people
the salvation which the risen Christ gives them,
let us pray to the Lord:

That Christ's message of peace to his disciples
will remove the pain of war and violence from human hearts,
let us pray to the Lord:

That people everywhere will use God's gifts of soil and water
according to God's plan, for the good of all,
let us pray to the Lord:

That we will recognize the risen Lord
in the breaking of the bread and wherever he reveals his presence,
let us pray to the Lord:

That those who have died,
especially _____ and _____,
will rejoice for ever in their risen Savior,
let us pray to the Lord:

+

+

Priest: God of our ancestors,
truly your voice speaks of peace:
peace for us, your people,
and for all who turn to you in their hearts.
By this Eucharist,
strengthen us to be more zealous messengers
of your peace.
We ask this in the name of Jesus the Lord.
Amen.

FOURTH SUNDAY OF EASTER

Priest: Dearly beloved, how great is the love we share as God's children!
Placing our confidence in that love,
let us bring our prayers to the Father of Jesus and our Father;
let us ask for the salvation that God promises us in the risen Son.

Minister: That those who shepherd the holy church of God under persecution
will find courage in the name of Jesus Christ,
let us pray to the Lord:

That those baptized at Easter, especially our parishioners,
_____ and _____,
will find lasting joy in the name of Jesus Christ,
let us pray to the Lord:

That those discerning a vocation to the priesthood, diaconate, or consecrated life
will find guidance in the name of Jesus Christ,
let us pray to the Lord:

That those who suffer from injury or sickness
will find healing in the name of Jesus Christ,
let us pray to the Lord:

That those who lack sufficient food or adequate housing
will find bountiful help in the name of Jesus Christ,
let us pray to the Lord:

That those who have died,
especially _____ and _____,
will find eternal life in the name of Jesus
    Christ,
let us pray to the Lord:

+

+

Priest: Lord God, in the power of Jesus' name
we stand before you in fervent prayer.
Grant us and all your children
the salvation Christ won for us by his death
    and resurrection.
Keep us united as his flock,
and help us follow him to glory.
Let us see your face and share your life,
for ever and ever. Amen.

FIFTH SUNDAY OF EASTER

Priest: All our needs are known to God even before we ask.
But let us voice our humble prayers
as the Holy Spirit prompts us,
confident that we will receive from God's hands
whatever is right and good.

Minister: That the ministers of the church will live in Christ
by the fruit of their generous service,
let us pray to the Lord:

That the leaders of nations will live in Christ
by the fruit of justice and peace,
let us pray to the Lord:

That parents will live in Christ
by the fruit of their loving care for their families,
let us pray to the Lord:

That those suffering from sickness or poverty
will live in Christ
by the fruit of their likeness to him,
let us pray to the Lord:

That all who have died,
especially _____ and _____,
will live in Christ
by the fruit of their everlasting union with him,
let us pray to the Lord:

+

+

Priest: We praise you, O God, in this assembly of your people,
for your strong bond of love unites us to your risen Son.
Give us the help and consolation of the Holy Spirit,
so that we may love in deed and in truth.
We ask this through Jesus Christ, the Lord. Amen.

SIXTH SUNDAY OF EASTER

Priest: With all who revere the living God,
let us pray that the salvation which is ours in
the risen Christ
will reach the ends of the earth.

Minister: For missionaries in this and every land,
that they live in Christ's love
through their proclamation of God's
wondrous deeds,
let us pray to the Lord:

For those baptized at Easter,
especially _____ and _____,
that they live in Christ's love
through their baptismal share of the Spirit,
let us pray to the Lord:

For the sick,
especially _____ and _____,
that they live in Christ's love
through their restoration to health,
let us pray to the Lord:

For those soon to graduate,
that they live in Christ's love
through their service to the human family,
let us pray to the Lord:

For those who have died,
especially _____ and _____,
that they live for ever in Christ's love
through their salvation in his death and
    resurrection,
let us pray to the Lord:

+

+

Priest: God of love,
you have revealed your saving power to all
    nations
by showing us your kindness and faithfulness
in the risen Lord.
Grant us what we need to know you and love
    you.
Help us love one another as Christ loved us,
so that keeping his commandments may be
    our joy.
We ask this through Christ our Lord. Amen.

ASCENSION OF THE LORD
(celebrated in some places on Sunday)

Priest: Jesus Christ, ascended on high, fills the whole world with God's gifts.
Let us pray for our needs and the needs of all people.

Minister: That God's grace in Jesus Christ will equip the church's ministers
to build up the Body of Christ,
let us pray to the Lord:

That God's grace in Jesus Christ will lead all people
to care for the environment,
let us pray to the Lord:

That God's grace in Jesus Christ
will help farmers to plant their crops and nurture their growth,
let us pray to the Lord:

That God's grace in Jesus Christ
will empower us to assist the needy in our midst,
let us pray to the Lord:

That God's grace in Jesus Christ
will bring those who have died,
especially _____ and _____,
to share his glory in heaven,
let us pray to the Lord:

+

+

Priest: Giver of all good gifts,
renew us in your service by your surpassing
    power,
and keep us united to our Savior, Jesus Christ,
whose love reaches to the heavens
and whose goodness fills all people with
    blessing,
both now and for ever. Amen.

SEVENTH SUNDAY OF EASTER
(where the Ascension is celebrated on Thursday)

Priest: Because God remains in us and we in God,
let us confidently offer our prayers.

Minister: That all who minister to the members of the church
will share the Lord's kindness in their generous service,
let us pray to the Lord:

That all peoples and nations will receive the Lord's kindness
in lasting deliverance from war and injustice,
let us pray to the Lord:

That all who struggle with illness and addiction
will know the Lord's kindness in renewed hope,
let us pray to the Lord:

That we who celebrate this Easter season
will welcome the Lord's kindness in this holy Eucharist,
let us pray to the Lord:

That those who have died,
especially _____ and _____,
will celebrate the Lord's kindness in everlasting life,
let us pray to the Lord:

✢

✢

Priest: God of heaven and earth,
make perfect in us the love of your Son, Jesus Christ,
in answer to these prayers,
for we trust in his power to protect and save us,
both now and for ever. Amen.

PENTECOST

Priest: Let us ask to drink deeply of the Holy Spirit as we offer these prayers.

Minister: For the Body of Christ,
that we rejoice in the many workings of the Holy Spirit,
let us pray to the Lord:

For the citizens of all nations,
that they rejoice in peace from on high,
let us pray to the Lord:

For graduates,
that they rejoice in past accomplishments and welcome future challenges,
let us pray to the Lord:

For those who suffer the loss of health, employment, or security,
that they rejoice in God's power to save,
let us pray to the Lord:

For those who honored Jesus as Lord in this life
and have died in him,
especially _____ and _____,
that they rejoice for ever in heaven,
let us pray to the Lord:

+

+

Priest: Lord of all creation,
with the large crowd assembled on the first Pentecost
we marvel at your saving deeds in Jesus Christ.
Renew us and our world in answer to our prayers,
through the same Jesus Christ, our Lord.
Amen.

SECOND SUNDAY IN ORDINARY TIME

Priest: In the power of the Holy Spirit who dwells in our hearts,
let us present our needs to God in these petitions.

Minister: For the welfare of the holy churches of God,
and for the unity of the human family,
let us pray to the Lord:

For the well-being of this nation,
of our president and vice president,
and for the safety of all who serve and protect us,
let us pray to the Lord:

For mutual respect and understanding
between ethnic groups in our country and throughout the world,
let us pray to the Lord:

For the recovery of the sick
and for the deliverance of the oppressed,
let us pray to the Lord:

For the everlasting joy of those who have died,
especially _____ and _____,
let us pray to the Lord:

✢

✢

Priest: Be present to us, Lord our God,
as you were to Samuel;
reveal your Son, the Messiah, to us
as you revealed him to Andrew and Peter.
Show us your love in answer to our prayers,
so that we may glorify you in all things.
We ask this through Christ our Lord. Amen.

THIRD SUNDAY IN ORDINARY TIME

Priest: Let us present our needs to the Lord, the God of our salvation.

Minister: For Pope _____ and the leaders of all Christian churches,
that they guide us to unity in faith and love,
let us pray to the Lord:

For civil leaders, that they promote respect for the unborn,
let us pray to the Lord:

For those who are suffering in body, mind, or spirit,
that they place their trust in God's unending love,
let us pray to the Lord:

For those who have died,
especially _____ and _____,
that they celebrate the everlasting goodness of God,
let us pray to the Lord:

For our particular needs, which we now remember.

[*pause for silent prayer*]

For all our needs, let us pray to the Lord:

+

+

Priest: God of compassion,
with the apostles we hear the call of your Son.
Grant what we have asked in these prayers,
so that we may follow him with love
and celebrate life in his kingdom,
both now and for ever. Amen.

FOURTH SUNDAY IN ORDINARY TIME

Priest: Let us pray that our hearts will be free from evil
and filled with God's goodness in answer to these prayers.

Minister: That the grace of Christ
will free the church from hypocrisy and disunity,
let us pray to the Lord:

That the peace of Christ
will free all people from hatred and violence,
let us pray to the Lord:

That the courage of Christ
will free the sick and dying from their fears,
let us pray to the Lord:

That the power of Christ,
will free us from the spirit of pride, anger, and apathy,
let us pray to the Lord:

That the dying and rising of Christ
will free from their sins those who have died,
especially _____ and _____,
let us pray to the Lord:

✢

✢

Priest: **Lord God,
let your might remove from us
all that lifts itself up against Jesus Christ,
    your Holy One,
so that we may praise you with thanksgiving,
both now and for ever. Amen.**

FIFTH SUNDAY IN ORDINARY TIME

Priest: Calling upon our ever-gracious God,
let us pray for our needs and the needs of people everywhere.

Minister: That the saving power of God
will strengthen the church for words and deeds of service,
let us pray to the Lord:

That the saving power of God
will draw married couples to deeper love,
let us pray to the Lord:

That the saving power of God
will rescue the sick and the poor from their distress,
let us pray to the Lord:

That the saving power of God
will remove from our lives whatever is harmful
and give us whatever is helpful,
let us pray to the Lord:

That the saving power of God
will bring those who have died,
especially _____ and _____,
to the glory of the resurrection,
let us pray to the Lord:

+

+

Priest: **Saving God,
we ask you to answer these prayers,
so that we will faithfully proclaim your
 Gospel
and eagerly do your will.
We ask this through Christ our Lord. Amen.**

SIXTH SUNDAY IN ORDINARY TIME

Priest: Let us turn to the Lord in fervent prayer.

Minister: For those who are alienated from the community of the church,
let us pray to the Lord:

For those who are ignored or oppressed
by the powerful of this world,
let us pray to the Lord:

For those who are ill, hungry, or homeless,
let us pray to the Lord:

For those in any kind of trouble,
and for all who have asked our prayers,
let us pray to the Lord:

For those who have died,
especially _____ and _____,
let us pray to the Lord:

✝

✝

Priest: Merciful God, like the needy ones of old
we come from town and countryside
to seek the healing touch of your Son, Jesus
  Christ.
May he cleanse us of all evil
and claim us anew as your holy people.
We ask this through the same Christ our Lord.
  Amen.

SEVENTH SUNDAY IN ORDINARY TIME

Priest: Let us ask God's salvation for all in need, both in this community and through all the earth.

Minister: That Christians will know the Lord's power in living as the new creation, let us pray to the Lord:

That nations and peoples will know the Lord's power in all that leads to peace and justice, let us pray to the Lord:

That the sick and the poor will know the Lord's power in their deliverance from suffering, let us pray to the Lord:

That we who are assembled here will know the Lord's power in the enduring gift of the Holy Spirit, let us pray to the Lord:

That those who have died, especially _____ and _____, will know the Lord's power in fullness of joy, let us pray to the Lord:

+

+

Priest: Lord our God, how tremendous are your deeds,
how marvelous your works!
Refuse not our prayers,
for we trust in your Son's power to help and save us.
Yours be the praise and the glory, for ever and ever. Amen.

EIGHTH SUNDAY IN ORDINARY TIME

Priest: My sisters and brothers,
let us humbly bring our petitions before the
God of mercy.

Minister: That the Lord's faithful Word
will sustain all who follow Jesus Christ,
let us pray to the Lord:

That the Lord's guiding hand will direct our
public servants
along paths of justice and peace,
let us pray to the Lord:

That the Lord's salvation will speedily deliver
all people
from poverty, unemployment, starvation, and
disease,
let us pray to the Lord:

That the Lord's gift of the Eucharist, the
wedding feast of God's kingdom,
will bind us together in the new covenant of
reconciliation,
let us pray to the Lord:

That the Lord's everlasting love will embrace
those who have died,
especially _____ and _____,
let us pray to the Lord:

✛

✛

Priest: **God rich in mercy,
grant us what we need to live as your holy
 people,
those called to celebrate life with your son,
 Jesus Christ,
both now and for ever. Amen.**

NINTH SUNDAY IN ORDINARY TIME

Priest: In every darkness, Christ is our light.
In every weakness, Christ is our might.
Let us offer our petitions in his most sacred name.

Minister: That God's surpassing power in Christ the shepherd
will strengthen all who minister to God's people,
let us pray to the Lord:

That God's surpassing power in Christ the peacemaker
will direct the policies of all leaders of governments,
let us pray to the Lord:

That God's surpassing power in Christ the liberator
will deliver the homeless and unemployed from their distress,
let us pray to the Lord:

That God's surpassing power in Christ the healer
will restore the sick and the injured to wholeness,
let us pray to the Lord:

That God's surpassing power in Christ the
    life-giver
will raise up those who have died,
especially _____ and _____,
let us pray to the Lord:

+

+

Priest: O God, our help in every need,
show your surpassing power to us
and to those we have remembered in prayer,
so that a song of thankful praise will rise from
    every heart.
We ask this through Christ our Lord. Amen.

TENTH SUNDAY IN ORDINARY TIME

Priest: As brothers and sisters of the Lord Jesus,
we know that God is always attentive to the
voice of our supplication.
And so we confidently pray:

Minister: That Pope _____ and all the leaders of
the church
fulfill their ministry with courage,
let us pray to the Lord:

That our local, state, and national officials
serve their people with unselfish zeal,
let us pray to the Lord:

That graduates of our schools
continue their pursuit of truth, goodness, and
beauty,
let us pray to the Lord:

That tourists, vacationers, and those who care
for them
enjoy a summer that is safe and refreshing,
let us pray to the Lord:

That farmers and gardeners
receive good weather for growing and
harvesting their crops,
let us pray to the Lord:

That those who suffer in body, mind or spirit
know God's abundant mercy in their need,
let us pray to the Lord:

That those who have died in Christ,
especially _____ and _____,
know everlasting joy in his presence,
let us pray to the Lord:

+

+

Priest: Creator and sustainer of all,
multiply your blessings among us
in answer to our prayers,
so that our thanksgiving may abound for your
    glory,
through Jesus Christ, our Lord. Amen.

ELEVENTH SUNDAY IN ORDINARY TIME

Priest: Let us ask to know the Lord's kindness and faithfulness in these prayers.

Minister: For the welfare of the holy church of God
and for the well-being of the human family,
let us pray to the Lord:

For the elimination of disease, famine, and war,
and for the reconciliation of states and peoples,
let us pray to the Lord:

For the recovery of the sick
and for the deliverance of the oppressed,
let us pray to the Lord:

For seasonable weather, sufficient rainfall,
and bountiful harvests,
let us pray to the Lord:

For the consolation of the dying
and for the eternal happiness of those who have died,
especially _____ and _____,
let us pray to the Lord:

✛

✛

Priest: Rock of our strength,
we give you thanks
for your many gifts to us,
but we seek your kindness in all our needs.
Hear and answer the prayers we present to
 you this day,
for we make them in the name of your
 beloved Son,
Jesus Christ, who is Lord for ever and ever.
 Amen.

TWELFTH SUNDAY IN ORDINARY TIME

Priest: Let us ask God to increase our faith as we present our needs.

Minister: That all who believe in Jesus
will know the Lord's everlasting love in unity and peace,
let us pray to the Lord:

That the human family
will know the Lord's everlasting love
in deliverance from war, famine, and disease,
let us pray to the Lord:

That the ill and infirm
will know the Lord's everlasting love in our compassion,
let us pray to the Lord:

That fathers and mothers will know the Lord's everlasting love
in caring for one another and their children,
let us pray to the Lord:

That those who have died in Christ,
especially _____ and _____,
will know the Lord's everlasting love in his death and resurrection,
let us pray to the Lord:

✢

✢

Priest: God our strength,
with the disciples in the storm-tossed boat
we seek refuge in Jesus Christ,
who shows us your everlasting love.
May he come to our help in answer to these
 prayers,
and rescue us from our distress,
both now and for ever. Amen.

THIRTEENTH SUNDAY IN ORDINARY TIME

Priest: Let us present our prayers to the Lord, whose kindness is undying.

Minister: That the members of the church
will find renewed strength in God's love,
let us pray to the Lord:

That all nations and peoples
will find lasting peace in God's plan for this
    world,
let us pray to the Lord:

That the ill and infirm
will find abundant comfort in God's healing,
let us pray to the Lord:

That all who worship here
will find sure hope in God's promises,
let us pray to the Lord:

That those who have died,
especially _____ and _____,
will find everlasting joy in God's salvation,
let us pray to the Lord:

✢

✢

Priest: All-holy God, you are merciful and gracious
　　　　　to us
and to all your people.
Look upon us in your great love,
and grant us the riches of your favor,
through Jesus Christ, our Lord. Amen.

FOURTEENTH SUNDAY IN ORDINARY TIME

Priest: Lifting our eyes to the God of mercy,
let us ask that the power of Christ
may rest upon us and upon our world.

Minister: For the church,
that it proclaim the Gospel with boldness,
let us pray to the Lord:

For civic leaders,
that they guide us in creating a more humane
world,
let us pray to the Lord:

For families,
that they find strength in sharing their joys
and sorrows,
let us pray to the Lord:

For ourselves,
that we take courage in the promises of Christ,
let us pray to the Lord:

For those who have died,
especially _____ and _____,
that they rejoice for ever in the company of
the saints,
let us pray to the Lord:

\+

\+

Priest: Show us your mercy, O Lord,
and grant us your saving help.
Increase our faith, so that your wondrous
 deeds in Christ Jesus
may abound in our midst.
We ask this through the same Christ our Lord.
 Amen.

FIFTEENTH SUNDAY IN ORDINARY TIME

Priest: Let us ask God's loving-kindness for ourselves and for all in need.

Minister: That Christians will know the Lord's salvation
in living as God's holy ones,
let us pray to the Lord:

That nations and peoples will know the Lord's salvation
in all that promotes care for the environment,
let us pray to the Lord:

That the poor and the oppressed will know the Lord's salvation
in their deliverance from suffering,
let us pray to the Lord:

That we who have been chosen in Christ Jesus
will know the Lord's salvation in this Eucharist,
let us pray to the Lord:

That those who have died,
especially _____ and _____,
will know the Lord's salvation in fullness of joy,
let us pray to the Lord:

✢

✢

Priest: **Generous God, grant us your salvation
in answer to these prayers,
for we make them in the name of your
    beloved Son,
Jesus Christ, who is Lord for ever and ever.
    Amen.**

SIXTEENTH SUNDAY IN ORDINARY TIME

Priest: Let us present our needs to God, the source of every blessing,
that we may proclaim the goodness of God's name
and glory in God's praise.

Minister: That the leaders of the church
will hear the Good Shepherd's voice
and receive his guidance,
let us pray to the Lord:

That rulers of nations will hear his voice
and receive his message of justice and peace,
let us pray to the Lord:

That those who are suffering from poverty
and illness will hear his voice
and receive his loving care,
let us pray to the Lord:

That the members of this community will hear his voice
and receive his renewing Spirit,
let us pray to the Lord:

That those who have died,
especially _____ and _____,
will hear his voice
and receive his everlasting joy,
let us pray to the Lord:

+

+

Priest: Father,
your Son speaks to us with a shepherd's love
 and authority
as he gives us the words of your mouth.
In the power of your Holy Spirit,
we ask you to answer our prayers,
so that we may greet your blessings with
 thanksgiving.
We make this prayer through Christ our Lord.
 Amen.

SEVENTEENTH SUNDAY IN ORDINARY TIME

Priest: The Lord Jesus took borrowed loaves and fishes
and made of them a meal to satisfy the hungry.
We, too, hunger for the rich food of God's love,
and so we bring our prayers before the God and Father of all.

Minister: That the leaders of the church
will heed the voice of God's Son,
and will bring his life-giving Word to others,
let us pray to the Lord:

That civil leaders will recognize the needs of the hungry, the poor, and the exploited,
and will share our land's abundance with them,
let us pray to the Lord:

That the sick and the suffering will receive many blessings
from the hand of the Lord,
and will rejoice in God's goodness,
let us pray to the Lord:

That we will use the talents which God has given us,
and will serve our sisters and brothers in humility,
let us pray to the Lord:

That those who have died,
especially _____ and _____,
will know the fullness of salvation in Christ
    Jesus
and will celebrate his love for ever,
let us pray to the Lord:

+

+

Priest: God and Father of all,
we ask you to transform us like the loaves
    and fishes,
so that we may be as nourishing for our
    brothers and sisters
as the holy gifts we share in this meal.
We ask this through Jesus Christ, our Lord.
    Amen.

EIGHTEENTH SUNDAY IN ORDINARY TIME

Priest: With faith in the One whom God has sent to us, let us bring our needs to our almighty Father.

Minister: That God's Son will give his guidance to the members of the church,
let us pray to the Lord:

That Jesus will give his peace to all peoples and nations,
let us pray to the Lord:

That Christ will give his consolation to the suffering and bereaved,
let us pray to the Lord:

That our Savior will give the bread of life to us for our salvation,
let us pray to the Lord:

That the risen Lord will give everlasting life to those who have died,
especially _____ and _____,
let us pray to the Lord:

Let us remember our personal intentions.

[*pause for silent prayer*]

That our Savior will give us help in every need,
let us pray to the Lord:

✢

✢

Priest: Holy and immortal God, you have set your
 seal on Christ
and have made him the source of life.
Hear our prayers for new and more abundant
 life in him,
this day and every day, both now and for ever.
 Amen.

NINETEENTH SUNDAY IN ORDINARY TIME

Priest: Together let us seek the Lord as we offer our petitions,
and take refuge in the Lord's loving-kindness.

Minister: That the ministers of the church will taste the Lord's goodness
in their service to God's people,
let us pray to the Lord:

That international organizations will taste the Lord's goodness
in their efforts for peace and justice,
let us pray to the Lord:

That the poor will taste the Lord's goodness
in our generous works of charity,
let us pray to the Lord:

That we who worship here will taste the Lord's goodness
on our journey to God's dwelling-place,
let us pray to the Lord:

That those who have died,
especially _____ and _____,
will taste the Lord's goodness in the gift of eternal life,
let us pray to the Lord:

✢

✢

Priest: Lord God, your Son leads us on the way of love.
Draw us to him in this Eucharist,
so that we may rejoice in him now,
and live with him in your presence,
for ever and ever. Amen.

TWENTIETH SUNDAY IN ORDINARY TIME

Priest: Let us ask God, our protector, to be mindful of us in our need
and strengthen us to do all that is good.

Minister: For those who lead the churches,
that they be enlightened to discern the way to Christian unity,
let us pray to the Lord:

For national and local government officials,
that they seek peace and follow after it,
let us pray to the Lord:

For the poor and the lowly,
that they be gladdened by many signs of God's care for them,
let us pray to the Lord:

For the members of this assembly,
that we take delight in Christ's gift of himself in the Eucharist,
let us pray to the Lord:

For those who have died,
especially _____ and _____,
that they render God eternal thanksgiving in heaven,
let us pray to the Lord:

✢

✢

Priest: Lord our God,
nothing is lacking to those who love you.
As we advance along the way of your truth,
nourish us with your living Word and living
    bread,
our Lord Jesus Christ.
Glory to him who is one with you and
    remains with us,
for ever and ever. Amen.

TWENTY-FIRST SUNDAY IN ORDINARY TIME

Priest: Let us call upon the Lord,
who has freed us from slavery to sin,
and ask strength to follow the Lord with all our hearts.

Minister: That Pope _____, the clergy, and religious
will serve the Lord with courage,
let us pray to the Lord:

That those who hold public office
will honor the Lord by their defense of human rights,
let us pray to the Lord:

That husbands and wives will glorify the Lord
by their love for each other,
let us pray to the Lord:

That we who have come to Jesus in this Eucharist
will bless the Lord in our words and deeds,
let us pray to the Lord:

That those who have died,
especially _____ and _____,
will praise the Lord in the glory of heaven,
let us pray to the Lord:

✢

✢

Priest: **Lord God,**
our needs are great and our troubles are many,
but your love for us is far greater.
Rescue us from all our distress
for the sake of him who redeemed our lives,
our Lord Jesus Christ.
Give us lasting joy in his words and food of
eternal life,
both now and for ever. Amen.

TWENTY-SECOND SUNDAY IN ORDINARY TIME

Priest: Let us call upon the Lord, who is close to us in every need.

Minister: That the Lord's goodness
will empower the members of the church for generous service,
let us pray to the Lord:

That the Lord's guidance
will direct our public servants along the paths of justice and peace,
let us pray to the Lord:

That the Lord's salvation
will deliver the people of this and every country
from poverty, starvation, and homelessness,
let us pray to the Lord:

That the Lord's compassion
will comfort the sick, the elderly, and the dying,
let us pray to the Lord:

That the Lord's mercy
will embrace the lives of those who have died,
especially _____ and _____,
let us pray to the Lord:

+

+

Priest: Father of lights, from whom every good gift comes,
answer our prayers in your great love.
Grant us whatever will help us to live in your presence,
and show us how to possess your promised land,
for ever and ever. Amen.

TWENTY-THIRD SUNDAY IN ORDINARY TIME

Priest: Let us pray with confidence to God,
whose faithfulness is seen in answer to our prayers.

Minister: That the leaders of the church will hear God's voice
and proclaim the Gospel with power,
let us pray to the Lord:

That rulers of nations will hear God's voice
and do God's will,
let us pray to the Lord:

That those who are suffering from illness and poverty
will hear God's voice and receive God's compassion,
let us pray to the Lord:

That we will hear God's voice and welcome
our share in God's kingdom,
let us pray to the Lord:

That those who have died,
especially _____ and _____,
will hear God's voice and celebrate God's salvation,
let us pray to the Lord:

✢

✢

Priest: **Liberating God,
we ask you to answer our prayers.
Let us grow more deeply open to you
through Jesus Christ, both now and for ever.
Amen.**

TWENTY-FOURTH SUNDAY IN ORDINARY TIME

Priest: Gathered together in Christ as sisters and brothers,
let us call to mind God's many blessings,
and ask God to answer our prayers.

Minister: For _____, our Pope; _____, our (arch)bishop;
all the church's ministers,
and the people they have been called to lead and serve,
let us pray to the Lord:

For those who serve in public office;
for legislators and judges;
and for all those entrusted with the common good,
let us pray to the Lord:

For those who are weakened by sin and sickness,
and for victims of famine and natural disaster throughout the world,
let us pray to the Lord:

For all of us gathered here in faith, reverence, and love of God,
and for all our parishioners,
let us pray to the Lord:

For those who have died,
especially _____ and _____,
let us pray to the Lord:

For our particular intentions, which we now remember.

[pause for silent prayer]

For these, let us pray to the Lord:

✝

✝

Priest: **Merciful God,
we ask you to answer us in our need,
and fill us with your saving grace,
through Jesus Christ, our Lord. Amen.**

TWENTY-FIFTH SUNDAY IN ORDINARY TIME

Priest: United in the Spirit who helps us to pray rightly,
let us ask the Lord to give us and all people whatever is for our good.

Minister: That the Lord will show great care for leaders of the church,
and sustain them in their call to humble service,
let us pray to the Lord:

That the Lord will show great care for our parish catechists,
and guide them in their ministry,
let us pray to the Lord:

That the Lord will show great care for the victims of injustice and prejudice,
and rescue them from their foes,
let us pray to the Lord:

That the Lord will show great care for the dead,
especially _____ and _____,
and raise them up to eternal life,
let us pray to the Lord:

Let us ask the Lord to show great care for us
as we remember our needs.

[*pause for silent prayer*]

That the Lord will give us whatever is helpful
and defend us from whatever is harmful,
let us pray to the Lord:

+

+

Priest: Lord God, great and everlasting is your care
for us.
Receive these prayers we have made to you,
and answer them for the sake of your beloved
Son, Jesus Christ,
who is Lord for ever and ever. Amen.

TWENTY-SIXTH SUNDAY IN ORDINARY TIME

Priest: Our help in every need is from the Lord.
In the power of the Holy Spirit,
let us offer these petitions to the God who upholds our lives.

Minister: That all the members of the church
may find renewed strength in Christ the Savior,
let us pray to the Lord:

That nations and peoples
may embrace lasting reconciliation in Christ the peacemaker,
let us pray to the Lord:

That teachers and students may savor abundant wisdom
in Christ the teacher,
let us pray to the Lord:

That those who suffer from sickness and poverty,
from injustice and violence,
may obtain speedy deliverance in Christ the liberator,
let us pray to the Lord:

That those who have died,
especially _____ and _____,
may put on everlasting glory in Christ the life-giver,
let us pray to the Lord:

Let us ask to receive from the Lord what we need this day.

[*pause for silent prayer*]

For all our needs, let us pray to the Lord:

✢

✢

Priest: **In your great love, answer us, O God, with your help that never fails. Yours be the praise and the glory through Jesus Christ, for ever and ever. Amen.**

TWENTY-SEVENTH SUNDAY IN ORDINARY TIME

Priest: The Lord God is our help in time of need.
Let us join our voices to ask the Lord's blessing
on ourselves and on all people.

Minister: For ministers of this local church and of all Christian churches,
that they follow Christ in his work of salvation,
let us pray to the Lord:

For public officials of this community, state, and nation,
that they defend the sacredness of human life in word and deed,
let us pray to the Lord:

For wives, husbands, and their children,
that they respect and cherish one another in mutual love,
let us pray to the Lord:

For the poor, the hungry, and the oppressed,
that they find deliverance in our acts of service,
let us pray to the Lord:

For the sick and victims of violence,
that they know Christ's embrace in their
    sufferings,
let us pray to the Lord:

For those who have died,
especially _____ and _____,
that they celebrate everlasting life in the reign
    of God,
let us pray to the Lord:

+

+

Priest: Lord God, source of every blessing,
lead us in the ways of your holiness
and consecrate us for your service,
through Jesus Christ, our Lord. Amen.

TWENTY-EIGHTH SUNDAY IN ORDINARY TIME

Priest: Because we know all things are possible with God,
let us offer fervent prayer for ourselves and for the whole world.

Minister: May the gracious care of the Lord
be with all who follow Christ.
For this, let us pray to the Lord:

May the gracious care of the Lord
be with those who govern communities and nations.
For this, let us pray to the Lord:

May the gracious care of the Lord
be with those who suffer from poverty, disease, and homelessness.
For this, let us pray to the Lord:

May the gracious care of the Lord
be with us who worship here.
For this, let us pray to the Lord:

May the gracious care of the Lord
be with those who have died,
especially _____ and _____.
For this, let us pray to the Lord:

✝

✝

Priest: God of all kindness,
we ask you to fill us with your love
as we seek your wisdom.
Let your saving work bring us to share your glory
in everlasting life.
We make this prayer through Christ our Lord.
Amen.

TWENTY-NINTH SUNDAY IN ORDINARY TIME

Priest: Placing our trust in the Lord,
let us confidently approach the throne of grace with our prayers.

Minister: That the Lord will show kindness to Christian missionaries
throughout the world,
and sustain them in their call to humble service,
let us pray to the Lord:

That the Lord will show kindness to rulers of nations
and preserve them from self-righteousness,
let us pray to the Lord:

That the Lord will show kindness to victims of famine and disease,
and grant them help in their need,
let us pray to the Lord:

That the Lord will show kindness to those who have died,
especially _____ and _____,
and deliver them from death,
let us pray to the Lord:

That the Lord will show kindness to us
as we remember our particular intentions.

[*pause for silent prayer*]

That the Lord will show us the abundance of
   divine favor,
let us pray to the Lord:

+

+

Priest: Lord God, Father of Jesus Christ,
you are gracious and merciful to all your
   people.
Hear us as we call upon you this day,
and help us to share the sacrifice of your Son,
   Jesus Christ,
who is Lord for ever and ever. Amen.

THIRTIETH SUNDAY IN ORDINARY TIME

Priest: Let us embrace the power of Christ's sacrifice for our sins,
and ask its saving grace for ourselves and for all people in these prayers.

Minister: For Christians throughout the world,
let us pray to the Lord:

For heads of governments, legislators, and judges,
let us pray to the Lord:

For those who suffer from physical or spiritual blindness,
let us pray to the Lord:

For the sick and the dying,
let us pray to the Lord:

For those who serve the needs of others,
let us pray to the Lord:

For those who have died in the peace of Christ,
especially _____ and _____,
let us pray to the Lord:

✝

✝

Priest: Lord God, with Bartimaeus, the blind man,
we take courage in calling out to you in our
   need.
Answer our prayers for the sake of him
in whom we believe and in whom we are
   saved,
Jesus Christ, who is Lord for ever and ever.
   Amen.

THIRTY-FIRST SUNDAY IN ORDINARY TIME

Priest: Let us ask to know the saving power of Jesus Christ
in answer to these prayers.

Minister: That the Lord Jesus will be the strength
of all who serve the community of believers,
let us pray to the Lord:

That the Lord Jesus will be the stronghold
of all who work for justice and peace,
let us pray to the Lord:

That the Lord Jesus will be a rock of refuge
for all who suffer from hunger, disease, and homelessness,
let us pray to the Lord:

That the Lord Jesus will be a fortress
for us in every struggle,
let us pray to the Lord:

That the Lord Jesus will be the salvation of all who have died,
especially _____ and _____,
let us pray to the Lord:

+

+

Priest: God of mercy,
we ask you to answer these prayers
that spring from our faith in you
and our love for you.
Renew within us the love that Jesus Christ
 showed to all in need.
We ask this through the same Christ our Lord.
 Amen.

THIRTY-SECOND SUNDAY IN ORDINARY TIME

Priest: In company with Christ,
who appears before the Father on our behalf,
let us offer fervent prayer for our needs
and those of the whole world.

Minister: That the church of God will have peace and unity
in this and every land,
let us pray to the Lord:

That those who serve in public office
will work for the well-being of all people,
let us pray to the Lord:

That those who are bowed down with hunger, sickness, and poverty
will be raised up by the Lord working through us,
let us pray to the Lord:

That we who assemble here to share the Lord's sacrifice
will receive his promised salvation,
let us pray to the Lord:

That all who have died,
especially _____ and _____,
will celebrate Christ's victory over death in his kingdom,
let us pray to the Lord:

✢

✢

Priest: Lord our God, your mercy is measureless,
and your love is beyond words to describe.
Look upon us in your loving-kindness,
and grant us the riches of your favor.
We ask this through Christ our Lord. Amen.

THIRTY-THIRD SUNDAY IN ORDINARY TIME

Priest: **Believing that the Lord is near, with us and within us,
we find new courage to pray:**

Minister: **For Pope _____ and for all church leaders,
let us pray to the Lord:**

**For national, state, and local officials,
let us pray to the Lord:**

**For those who suffer from any need,
let us pray to the Lord:**

**For those who have died,
especially _____ and _____,
let us pray to the Lord:**

**For those who have asked our prayers,
whom we now remember.**

[pause for silent prayer]

For these people, let us pray to the Lord:

✝

✝

Priest: **Lord God, hope of all in need,**
we ask you to answer our prayers.
Keep us safe in your love,
this day and on the final day.
We ask this in the name of Jesus, your Son,
who will be revealed as the Lord of power and
   glory,
for ever and ever. Amen.

OUR LORD JESUS CHRIST THE KING

Priest: The crucified Lord is the faithful witness
to the reign of God in this world.
In his most sacred name,
let us offer our prayers to the God of majesty.

Minister: For the church,
that it lead all peoples and nations
to serve Jesus Christ the King,
let us pray to the Lord:

For the leaders of nations and governments,
that God's truth shape their policies and
 actions
for the good of all,
let us pray to the Lord:

For those who suffer illness, poverty and
 oppression,
that the love of God in Jesus Christ
rescue them from harm,
let us pray to the Lord:

For us, God's royal and priestly people,
that we embrace our baptismal call to
 holiness,
let us pray to the Lord:

For those who have died,
especially _____ and _____,
that Jesus Christ, the firstborn of the dead,
welcome them to their eternal home,
let us pray to the Lord:

┼

┼

Priest: Lord our God, by our prayers,
establish your rule more fully in our hearts
    and in our world,
and help us to welcome your Son, Jesus
    Christ,
whose glorious kingdom we hope to share, for
    ever and ever. Amen.

THE MOST HOLY TRINITY

Priest: Our needs are great, but God's love for us is far greater.
Let us offer these petitions to the God who has made us a holy people.

Minister: That God will be glorified
in efforts for unity in this local church and in the universal church,
let us pray to the Lord:

That God will be glorified
in work for peace and justice among nations and peoples,
let us pray to the Lord:

That God will be glorified
in the healing of all who suffer in body, mind, or spirit,
let us pray to the Lord:

That God will be glorified
in our embrace of God's loving-kindness,
let us pray to the Lord:

That God will be glorified
in the gift of everlasting life to all who have died,
especially _____ and _____,
let us pray to the Lord:

+

+

Priest: Abba, Father,
your Holy Spirit gives us confidence
in your unending love for us,
so we cry out to you in these prayers.
Answer them for the sake of your Son, Jesus Christ,
in whom we have life in the land of your glory,
for ever and ever. Amen.

THE MOST HOLY BODY AND BLOOD OF CHRIST

Priest: Let us call on the name of the Lord in these prayers.

Minister: That those who lead the churches
will help us live as the one Body of Christ,
let us pray to the Lord:

That national and local government officials
will satisfy the human hunger for peace and justice,
let us pray to the Lord:

That the sick and the hospitalized
will receive many signs of divine and human love for them,
let us pray to the Lord:

That this assembly will delight in Christ's gift of himself
in the Eucharist,
let us pray to the Lord:

That those who have died,
especially _____ and _____,
will share Christ's eternal banquet in heaven,
let us pray to the Lord:

✝

✝

Priest: God of the covenant,
you accepted the sacrifice of your beloved Son,
who entered the heavenly sanctuary with his precious Blood.
Answer our prayers,
and give us hearts as generous and loving as his,
so that we may share the bread of life and the cup of salvation with thanksgiving.
We ask this through Christ our Lord. Amen.

THE MOST SACRED HEART OF JESUS

Priest: In the Most Sacred Heart of Jesus are found all the treasures of God's love.
Let us ask to share these riches in answer to our prayers.

Minister: That the church will receive the riches of divine holiness
in the Heart of Jesus,
let us pray to the Lord:

That the peoples of the world
will receive the riches of divine peace
in the Heart of Jesus,
let us pray to the Lord:

That those who share the sufferings of the crucified Lord
in their sickness, poverty, and loneliness
will receive the riches of divine consolation
in the Heart of Jesus,
let us pray to the Lord:

That we who celebrate God's saving plan in this Eucharist
will receive the riches of divine love
in the Heart of Jesus,
let us pray to the Lord:

That those who have died,
especially _____ and _____,
will receive the riches of divine mercy
in the Heart of Jesus,
let us pray to the Lord:

✛

✛

Priest: Father, Holy One,
let us draw water joyfully from the spring of salvation
that flows from the Heart of your beloved Son, Jesus Christ,
and grant us your merciful love in him,
both now and for ever. Amen.

December 8

THE IMMACULATE CONCEPTION OF THE BLESSED VIRGIN MARY

Priest: **In company with the sinless Virgin Mary, the Mother of all who are alive in Christ, let us offer our petitions.**

Minister: **That all Christians will know God's marvelous deeds in their adoption as God's children, let us pray to the Lord:**

That the people of the United States, entrusted to immaculate Mary's patronage, will know God's marvelous deeds in a renewal of their national life, let us pray to the Lord:

That the young and the elderly will know God's marvelous deeds in all that promotes their safety and well-being, let us pray to the Lord:

That we will know God's marvelous deeds in abundant help for every difficulty, let us pray to the Lord:

That those who have died, especially _____ and _____, will know God's marvelous deeds in life for ever with Mary and all the saints, let us pray to the Lord:

+

+

Priest: **All-holy God,
we ask you to make your salvation known to
 us today
in answer to these prayers.
Accomplish your will in us and through us,
so that, with Mary, we may praise your glory
in her Son, Jesus Christ,
who is Lord for ever and ever. Amen.**

December 12

OUR LADY OF GUADALUPE
(United States of America)

Priest: With a mother's love,
the Blessed Virgin Mary intercedes for us
and for all the peoples of the Americas.
Let us join our prayers to hers in these
petitions.

Minister: For the church,
for whom Mary, most admirable Mother,
is the pattern of holiness,
let us pray to the Lord:

For the people of Mexico,
for whom Our Lady of Guadalupe is a bringer
of hope and consolation,
let us pray to the Lord:

For the lowly of the earth,
and the afflicted in body, mind, or spirit,
for whom the most powerful Virgin is their
comforter,
let us pray to the Lord:

For us who worship here,
for whom the most faithful Virgin is our
example of discipleship,
let us pray to the Lord:

For those who have died,
especially _____ and _____,
for whom the most merciful Virgin is the gate
    of heaven,
let us pray to the Lord:

+

+

Priest: God of all the earth,
Elizabeth, the mother of John the Baptist,
marveled that her cousin Mary should come
    to her.
On this festival day,
we marvel that Our Lady of Guadalupe came
    to visit us.
Answer our prayers, we humbly ask,
so that we may share Mary's joy
in proclaiming your greatness,
both now and for ever. Amen.

January (third Monday)

MARTIN LUTHER KING, JR., HOLIDAY
(United States of America)

Priest: As we honor the Reverend Doctor Martin Luther King, Jr.,
let us pray for the grace to believe what he taught
and to practice what we believe.

Minister: For Jews, Christians, Muslims, and all people of faith,
that God may lead them to mutual love and unity,
let us pray to the Lord:

For our civil authorities, for legislators and judges,
that God may direct their hearts and minds
to work for justice and equality,
let us pray to the Lord:

For the poor, the exploited, and the persecuted,
that God may empower us to assist them in their need,
let us pray to the Lord:

For ourselves,
that God may strengthen us
to embrace the liberating power of the Gospel,
let us pray to the Lord:

For those who have died,
especially martyrs in the struggle for civil and human rights,
that God may bring them to a place of everlasting peace,
let us pray to the Lord:

+

+

Priest: Lord God almighty,
as we remember your merciful love in Jesus Christ,
we sing our "hallelujahs" for Reverend Martin Luther King, Jr.,
and we ask that there be plenty good room in your kingdom
for us and for all your children,
through the same Christ our Lord. Amen.

March 19

ST. JOSEPH, HUSBAND OF THE BLESSED VIRGIN MARY

Priest: In company with Saint Joseph,
whose fatherly care surrounded the child Jesus,
let us confidently pray for the needs of our church
and of our world.

Minister: That the ministers of the church
will celebrate God's everlasting kindness
by proclaiming the Gospel of salvation
through faith in Jesus Christ,
let us pray to the Lord:

That nations and peoples
will celebrate God's enduring faithfulness
by embracing all that leads to lasting peace,
let us pray to the Lord:

That the sick and injured, the poor and the oppressed,
will celebrate God's infinite compassion
by rejoicing in speedy deliverance from their suffering,
let us pray to the Lord:

That we who worship here
and all of Abraham's descendants
will celebrate God's eternal covenant
by speaking and acting in righteousness,
let us pray to the Lord:

That all who have died,
especially _____ and _____,
will celebrate God's infinite mercy
by living for ever in God's house,
let us pray to the Lord:

+

+

Priest: **All praise be yours, God of holy Mary and
Saint Joseph,
for giving us a place in your kingdom.
We join our prayers to theirs,
and ask to know your goodness in Jesus Christ,
the son of David,
for ever and ever. Amen.**

March 25

THE ANNUNCIATION OF THE LORD

Priest: In the Virgin Mary's Son, Jesus Christ,
we receive the joyful announcement
of God's saving plan for us.
Let us pray for its fulfillment in the church,
in the world, and in human hearts.

Minister: That God will be with our Holy Father, our (arch)bishop,
our pastor, and deacon(s) in their ministry,
let us pray to the Lord:

That God will be with all Christians
in their witness to the Gospel,
let us pray to the Lord:

That God will be with the rulers of nations
in their decisions and actions,
let us pray to the Lord:

That God will be with us who worship here
in our discipleship,
let us pray to the Lord:

That God will be with those who have died,
especially _____ and _____,
in their life with Christ for ever,
let us pray to the Lord:

+

+

Priest: Lord God,
we celebrate the power of your grace in the
 Blessed Virgin Mary
and in us, her children.
Deepen our love for you and for others
as we seek to do your will more completely.
We ask this through Christ our Lord. Amen.

MEMORIAL DAY
(United States of America)

Priest: **The Lord Jesus Christ, victor over death, powerfully intercedes for the living and the dead.
Let us join our prayers to his on this day of remembrance.**

Minister: **For God's mercy upon all who believe in Jesus Christ,
let us pray to the Lord:**

**For an end to hatred and violence throughout the world,
let us pray to the Lord:**

**For the eternal happiness of those who have died,
especially those who gave their lives in defense of our country,
let us pray to the Lord:**

**For the healing of the sick and the deliverance of the oppressed,
let us pray to the Lord:**

**For grace to walk the way of discipleship and share everlasting life with all the saints,
let us pray to the Lord:**

✢

✢

Priest: God of compassion,
hear our prayers for our departed brothers and sisters
who trusted in Jesus, your beloved Son.
Bring us all together into your kingdom of light and peace,
where Jesus is Lord, for ever and ever. Amen.

June 24

THE NATIVITY OF ST. JOHN THE BAPTIST

Priest: With John the Baptist, herald of the Messiah, let us pray that God's salvation in Jesus Christ will reach the ends of the earth.

Minister: That the all-seeing God
will raise up zealous prophets in the church,
let us pray to the Lord:

That the all-caring God
will lead the nations in the ways of justice
    and peace,
let us pray to the Lord:

That the all-compassionate God
will rescue the suffering from their distress,
let us pray to the Lord:

That the all-powerful God
will strengthen us to prepare the way of the
    Lord,
let us pray to the Lord:

That the all-merciful God
will gather those who have died,
especially _____ and _____,
into God's kingdom,
let us pray to the Lord:

+

+

Priest: God of saints and sinners,
wonderful are your works in the life of John
    the Baptist
and in our lives.
You fully know us and our needs,
and so we ask to see your salvation
in answer to these prayers,
both now and for ever. Amen.

June 29

SAINT PETER AND SAINT PAUL, APOSTLES

Priest: With Saint Peter and Saint Paul, witnesses to Jesus Christ in life and in death,
let us call upon our faithful God in these prayers.

Minister: That God's wisdom will guide the ministry of Pope _____, the successor of Peter;
of our (arch)bishop; and of all who serve the church,
let us pray to the Lord:

That God's love will unite all Christians
in the one, holy, catholic, and apostolic church,
let us pray to the Lord:

That God's goodness will bless people and parishes
that bear the names of Saints Peter and Paul,
let us pray to the Lord:

That God's peace will reconcile states and peoples,
especially in the lands where Saints Peter and Paul preached,
let us pray to the Lord:

That God's providence will gladden farmers and gardeners
with gentle rains and plentiful crops,
let us pray to the Lord:

That God's mercy will raise up to eternal
     happiness
those who have died,
especially _____ and _____,
let us pray to the Lord:

Let us commend ourselves and one another to
     almighty God
as we remember our needs.

[*pause for silent prayer*]

That God's care will help, save, and defend us,
let us pray to the Lord:

+

+

Priest: God of glory, your risen Son commissioned
     his chosen apostles
to preach the good news to all creation.
Strengthen us with apostolic teaching,
and empower us to be your witnesses
in what we say and do.
We make this prayer through Jesus Christ, our
     Lord. Amen.

July 4

INDEPENDENCE DAY
(United States of America)

Priest: On this Independence Day,
let us ask to know the saving power of Jesus Christ
in answer to these prayers.

Minister: That the Lord Jesus will be the strength
of all who lead the churches in our country,
let us pray to the Lord:

That the Lord Jesus will be the stronghold
of all who serve and defend us,
let us pray to the Lord:

That the Lord Jesus will be the protection
of all who suffer from hunger, disease, and homelessness,
let us pray to the Lord:

That the Lord Jesus will be the Savior for us
in every difficulty,
let us pray to the Lord:

That the Lord Jesus will be the joy of all who have died,
especially _____ and _____,
let us pray to the Lord:

+

+

Priest: God rich in mercy,
we ask you to answer these prayers
that spring from our faith in you and love for
  you.
Renew within the people of this nation
the love that Jesus Christ showed to all in
  need.
We ask this through the same Christ our Lord.
  Amen.

August 15

THE ASSUMPTION OF THE BLESSED VIRGIN MARY

Priest: Let us pray to our God,
who has willed that the glorious Virgin Mary
be praised in every generation.

Minister: With holy Mary,
who heard the Word of God and kept it,
let us ask the power of the Gospel
for the church's ministry.
For this, let us pray to the Lord:

With holy Mary,
who enclosed in her womb
him whom the world cannot contain,
let us ask peace for the peoples of the earth.
For this, let us pray to the Lord:

With holy Mary,
helper of the afflicted,
let us ask God's abundant gifts
for those in material or spiritual need.
For this, let us pray to the Lord:

With holy Mary,
foremost disciple of her Son,
let us ask deeper faith for all who worship
here.
For this, let us pray to the Lord:

With holy Mary,
taken body and soul into the glory of heaven,
let us ask everlasting life for those who have
 died,
especially _____ and _____.
For this, let us pray to the Lord:

+

+

Priest: **God of glory,
may the prayers of the Blessed Virgin Mary,
joined to ours,
obtain for us what we need this day,
and lead us to the joys of our heavenly home,
where Jesus is Lord, for ever and ever. Amen.**

September (first Monday)

LABOR DAY
(United States of America and Canada)

Priest: Let us raise our hearts and voices in prayer,
so that the Creator's generous gifts
will come to us through our work.

Minister: For the success of those called to ministry in the church,
let us pray to the Lord:

For safe working conditions and a just return for human labor,
let us pray to the Lord:

For compassionate care for the physical and spiritual needs of immigrants in our country,
let us pray to the Lord:

For wisdom and commitment to preserve the environment
that God has entrusted to us,
let us pray to the Lord:

For refreshing leisure and wholesome recreation,
let us pray to the Lord:

For the eternal joy of those who now rest in God,
especially _____ and _____,
let us pray to the Lord:

✛

✛

Priest: **Lord God, source of our strength,
prosper the work of our minds and hands,
so that your blessings will abound for us
and for all your people,
through Jesus Christ, our Lord. Amen.**

September 14

THE EXALTATION OF THE HOLY CROSS

Priest: The Lord Jesus humbled himself
and became obedient unto death,
even to death on a cross.
In the power of his resurrection from the dead,
let us pray that all people will be raised up
to new life in Christ the Lord.

Minister: Christ crucified became like us in our weakness;
through his Cross,
may the church become like him in his saving power.
For this, let us pray to the Lord:

Christ crucified became like the poor and the oppressed in their need;
through his Cross,
may they become like him in his triumph over injustice.
For this, let us pray to the Lord:

Christ crucified became like us in our sorrows;
through his Cross,
may all who suffer become like him in his lasting joy.
For this, let us pray to the Lord:

Christ crucified became like us in our human
    lowliness;
through his Cross,
may we become like him in his divine glory.
For this, let us pray to the Lord:

Christ crucified became like the dead in their
    emptiness;
through his Cross,
may those who have died,
especially _____ and _____,
become like him in his fullness of life.
For this, let us pray to the Lord:

+

+

Priest: Lord God,
answer our prayers in your great mercy,
so that the mystery of our redemption in the
    Cross of Christ
may transform us and the world you love.
We ask this through our crucified yet risen
    Savior,
Jesus Christ, who is Lord for ever and ever.
    Amen.

November 1

ALL SAINTS

Priest: Commemorating God's holy ones of every time and place,
and united with them in love for Jesus Christ,
let us join our prayers to theirs.

Minister: With the great Mother of God, Mary most-holy,
let us ask God's salvation for all her children.
For this, let us pray to the Lord:

With the holy apostles,
who preached the Gospel throughout the world,
let us ask God's loving-kindness for all nations and peoples.
For this, let us pray to the Lord:

With the white-robed company of martyrs,
who shed their blood for Christ,
let us ask God's strength for those persecuted for their faith.
For this, let us pray to the Lord:

With holy pastors and preachers,
who taught what they believed and lived what they taught,
let us ask God's wisdom for all who teach the Christian faith
by word and example.
For this, let us pray to the Lord:

With the souls of the just made perfect,
who placed their hope in Jesus Christ,
let us ask God's eternal happiness for those
    who have died,
especially _____ and _____.
For this, let us pray to the Lord:

+

+

Priest: God of blessedness,
grant us to share the holiness of your saints,
so that we may become true followers of your
    Son,
our Lord Jesus Christ,
who lives and reigns with you and the Holy
    Spirit,
one God, for ever and ever. Amen.

November 2

COMMEMORATION OF THE FAITHFUL DEPARTED
(All Souls)

Priest: **Let us call upon the God whose mercy does not forsake the living or the dead.**

Minister: **For the church, that it live in the power of the holy cross to save us, let us pray to the Lord:**

For victims of warfare, disease and starvation, that they share the triumph of the risen Christ, let us pray to the Lord:

For those who died suddenly through accident, tragedy, or natural disaster, that Jesus Christ welcome them to a place of everlasting peace, let us pray to the Lord:

For our parishioners who have fallen asleep in Christ during the past year:

[*names are read*]

That they rejoice for ever in the One who makes all things new, let us pray to the Lord:

For those who mourn,
that their tears be wiped away by the mystery
of the Lord's dying and rising,
let us pray to the Lord:

For our departed sisters and brothers whom
we remember in our hearts:

[*pause for silent prayer*]

That they receive everlasting joy and glory
with all the saints,
let us pray to the Lord:

+

+

Priest: Lord God,
mercifully grant your forgiveness
to our loved ones who have died.
Through our prayers,
may they obtain the pardon which they
always desired,
and celebrate eternal life with Jesus Christ,
who is Lord for ever and ever. Amen.

November 9

THE DEDICATION OF THE LATERAN BASILICA IN ROME

Priest: We are God's building,
the living stones rising on a firm foundation
   in Christ Jesus.
In the power of the Holy Spirit who dwells
   within us,
let us offer fervent prayers to the Lord.

Minister: That the church will gather into one
the scattered children of God throughout the
   world,
let us pray to the Lord:

That believers of all religions
will be able to worship God in freedom and
   peace,
let us pray to the Lord:

That architects, designers, and artists will use
   their talents
to reveal the glory of God,
let us pray to the Lord:

That we who render devoted service to God in
   this Eucharist
will render generous help to our needy
   brothers and sisters,
let us pray to the Lord:

That all who have died,
especially _____ and _____,
will find a dwelling place in God's eternal
    home,
let us pray to the Lord:

+

+

Priest: Lord God, wise builder of your church,
we ask you to answer the prayers
we have offered in your holy house.
Raise us to share the everlasting glory of your
    risen Son,
Jesus Christ, who is Lord for ever and ever.
    Amen.

THANKSGIVING DAY
(United States of America)

Priest: With gratitude to God for the many blessings that fill our lives,
let us ask for God's good gifts in abundance.

Minister: For the well-being of all who celebrate this day of feasting and leisure,
let us pray to the Lord:

For our creative vision and inventive skill
in the continuing work of creation,
let us pray to the Lord:

For all that sets people free from pain, fear, and hatred,
let us pray to the Lord:

For safe travel during this holiday weekend,
let us pray to the Lord:

For the grace to live as God's thankful people,
let us pray to the Lord:

For refreshment, light, and peace for the faithful departed,
especially _____ and _____,
let us pray to the Lord:

+

+

Priest: Lord God, we echo the cry of the leper in the gospel
as we ask your mercy,
and join our thanksgiving to his in this Eucharist.
Grant us whatever is for our good and your glory,
through Jesus Christ, our Lord. Amen.

Year C

FIRST SUNDAY OF ADVENT

Priest: As we begin the season of Advent, let us call upon God our Savior in fervent prayer.

Minister: That the Lord's guidance will be with the leaders of the church, let us pray to the Lord:

That the Lord's justice will be with the leaders of nations, let us pray to the Lord:

That the Lord's kindness will be with those who suffer from hunger and disease, let us pray to the Lord:

That the Lord's constancy will be with all who seek to do God's will, let us pray to the Lord:

That the Lord's friendship will be with all who have died, especially _____ and _____, let us pray to the Lord:

✢

✢

Priest: **Lord God,
let our prayers at this Eucharist
help us welcome your Son here in our midst
and at the end of time.
We ask this through Christ our Lord. Amen.**

SECOND SUNDAY OF ADVENT

Priest: The Lord Jesus is always near to us,
always coming into our hearts.
As we await the revelation of Christ's glory at
 the end of the ages,
let us ask God to hear and answer
 these petitions.

Minister: That the Lord will give wisdom
to those who promote the Gospel of Christ,
let us pray to the Lord:

That the Lord will give comfort
to those who live in mourning and misery,
let us pray to the Lord:

That the Lord will give healing
to those who are weakened by sin
 and sickness,
let us pray to the Lord:

That the Lord will give renewed strength
to us who are gathered here,
let us pray to the Lord:

That the Lord will give everlasting glory
to those who have died,
especially _____ and _____,
let us pray to the Lord:

✠

✠

Priest: Ruler of all times and seasons,
we ask you to fill these days of waiting with
 your saving love.
Deepen our love for you and for each other.
Bring us to glory with your Son, Jesus Christ,
who lives and reigns with you and the
 Holy Spirit,
one God, for ever and ever. Amen.

THIRD SUNDAY OF ADVENT

Priest: My brothers and sisters,
let us confidently present our needs to God
and ask God's promised salvation in
 these prayers.

Minister: For leaders of Christian churches
 and communities,
that the Lord's strength
will renew them in their responsibilities,
let us pray to the Lord:

For leaders of governments,
that the Lord's courage
will lead them along the ways of justice
 and peace,
let us pray to the Lord:

For the sick and injured,
that the Lord's peace
will stand guard over their lives,
let us pray to the Lord:

For babies about to be born,
that the Lord's care
will bring them to the fullness of
 their humanity,
let us pray to the Lord:

For this assembly of God's people,
that the Lord's presence
will make us a source of spiritual joy for
 each other,
let us pray to the Lord:

For those who have died,
especially _____ and _____,
that the Lord's salvation
will fill them with everlasting joy,
let us pray to the Lord:

+

+

Priest: God our Savior, let us draw water joyfully
from the springs of your mercy.
Let us see your greatness in answer to
    our prayers,
for we make them in the name of your Son,
    Jesus Christ,
who is Lord for ever and ever. Amen.

FOURTH SUNDAY OF ADVENT

Priest: Our help in every need is from the Lord.
In company with Christ,
let us pray to the God who upholds our lives.

Minister: That the Lord will give new life to the church
as it prepares for the return of its Lord,
let us pray to the Lord:

That the Lord will give new life
to rulers of nations and their people,
let us pray to the Lord:

That the Lord will give new life
to victims of injustice and persecution,
let us pray to the Lord:

That the Lord will give new life
to those who are crushed by poverty
 and illness,
let us pray to the Lord:

That the Lord will give new life
to those who have died,
especially _____ and _____,
let us pray to the Lord:

Let us remember our personal needs.

[pause for silent prayer]

That the Lord will give us new life
in every need,
let us pray to the Lord:

✢

✢

Priest: **Rouse your power, Lord,
in answer to our prayers.
As we turn away from trust in ourselves,
help us turn to trust in you,
the source of new life.
We ask this through Christ our Lord. Amen.**

December 24

CHRISTMAS EVE

Priest: God so loved the world
that God gave us the only-begotten Son;
in him we become heirs of eternal life as
   God's children.
As we joyfully celebrate God's salvation
made incarnate in Jesus Christ,
let us pray for its fulfillment in ourselves and
   in all people,
even to the ends of the earth.

Minister: That those who lead the church
will behold the salvation of our God
in their ministry of God's grace and mercy,
let us pray to the Lord:

That those who lead nations
will behold the salvation of our God
in their successful efforts for justice
   and peace,
let us pray to the Lord:

That those who suffer from sickness,
   unemployment, and poverty
will behold the salvation of our God
in words of hope and deeds of love,
let us pray to the Lord:

That those who are gathered here
will behold the salvation of our God
in their zeal for all that is right and just,
let us pray to the Lord:

That those who have died,
especially _____ and _____,
will behold the salvation of our God
in the Lord's kindness and faithfulness,
let us pray to the Lord:

+

+

Priest: Lord, our mighty God,
our gladness on this holy night is
　　great indeed,
for we find our everlasting light
in your Son who dwells with us.
In his name, we ask you to hear our prayers
and sustain us in your justice and constancy.
To you, Father, be all glory in the highest,
through Jesus Christ, our Savior,
in the power of the Holy Spirit,
both now and for ever. Amen.

December 25

CHRISTMAS DAY

Priest: **Christ is born!**
The reign of God dawns in our midst.
Let us ask that God's kindness and generous
    love in the Word made flesh
will fill the earth in answer to these prayers.

Minister: **For the faithfulness of God**
to make the church a holy people,
let us pray to the Lord:

For the peace of God
to gladden all nations on earth,
let us pray to the Lord:

For the comfort of God
to save those afflicted by any need,
especially _____ and _____,
let us pray to the Lord:

For the grace of God
to renew us and all believers in hope,
let us pray to the Lord:

For the glory of God
to fill those who have died,
especially _____ and _____,
let us pray to the Lord:

✛

✛

Priest: **Lord God,**
on this holy day we joyfully proclaim:
in every darkness, Christ our light!
in every weakness, Christ our might!
Let our prayers bring us your favor in him,
both now and for ever. Amen.

THE HOLY FAMILY OF JESUS, MARY, AND JOSEPH

Priest: As God's chosen ones,
made holy and beloved through Jesus Christ,
let us ask our Father to receive these prayers
for the human family

Minister: That the leaders of the church
will clothe themselves with Christ
by putting on his self-denial,
let us pray to the Lord:

That the leaders of nations
will clothe themselves with Christ
by putting on his humility,
let us pray to the Lord:

That families will clothe themselves
    with Christ
by putting on his kindness,
let us pray to the Lord:

That the suffering will clothe themselves
    with Christ
by putting on his patience,
let us pray to the Lord:

That we will clothe ourselves with Christ
by putting on his discipleship,
let us pray to the Lord:

That the dead, especially _____ and
_____,
will clothe themselves with Christ
by putting on the glory of his resurrection,
let us pray to the Lord:

+

+

Priest: **God of peace,
you have made us one family in Christ Jesus.
In his name,
we ask you to share with us and with all
 your people
the blessings of your incarnate Son.
Let your everlasting love
bind us close to him and to each other,
this day and every day,
both now and for ever. Amen.**

January 1

THE BLESSED VIRGIN MARY, THE MOTHER OF GOD

Priest: Now let us ask God's blessing upon the new year through Jesus Christ,
who has become one of us
in all things but sin.

Minister: Christ became like us in our weakness;
may the church become like him in his saving power.
For this, let us pray to the Lord:

Christ became like the poor and the oppressed in their suffering;
may they become like him in his triumph over injustice.
For this, let us pray to the Lord:

Christ became like us in our human lowliness;
may we become like him in his divine glory.
For this, let us pray to the Lord:

Christ became like the dead in their emptiness;
may those who have died,
especially _____ and _____,
become like him in his fullness of life.
For this, let us pray to the Lord:

Christ became like us in our need;
let us now remember our particular needs
on this day of beginnings.

[pause for silent prayer]

For these, let us pray to the Lord:

✢

✢

Priest: Lord God, with Mary, the Queen of Peace,
we treasure the fulfillment of your promises
    in our lives.
Help us to live as your sons and daughters
in the new year that you give us,
so that with the shepherds
we may praise and glorify you
for your kindness to us in your Son,
    Jesus Christ,
who is Lord for ever and ever. Amen.

SECOND SUNDAY AFTER CHRISTMAS
(where Epiphany is observed on January 6)

Priest: The Word of God, who was made flesh in Jesus Christ,
is the source of grace and truth for us and for all people.
Let us pray that God's gifts in Christ
will change darkness into light for all the world.

Minister: That God's wisdom may dwell in those
who serve the community of believers,
let us pray to the Lord:

That God's justice may dwell in those
who are entrusted with public office,
let us pray to the Lord:

That God's light may dwell in those
who are overshadowed by suffering and despair,
let us pray to the Lord:

That God's favor may dwell in us
who are gathered here,
let us pray to the Lord:

That God's glory may dwell in those
who have been called in death to an eternal inheritance,
especially _____ and _____,
let us pray to the Lord:

✢

✢

Priest: How wonderful are your works, Lord God!
In wisdom you have made them all.
Hear us as we pray for every
 spiritual blessing.
Dwell with us, live in us,
as we celebrate the birth of your beloved Son,
 Jesus Christ,
who is Lord for ever and ever. Amen.

THE EPIPHANY OF THE LORD

Priest: Let us raise our eyes to behold the
Father's glory
shining on the face of Christ,
and devoutly offer these petitions
for ourselves and all humanity.

Minister: That the leaders of the church will
reveal Christ
through their lives of simplicity and service,
let us pray to the Lord:

That the leaders of governments will
reveal Christ
through their assistance to exiles and refugees,
let us pray to the Lord:

That those in need of healing,
especially _____ and _____,
will reveal Christ
through their recovery from sickness,
let us pray to the Lord:

That the members of this assembly will
reveal Christ
through their renewed dedication to
his Gospel,
let us pray to the Lord:

That all those who have died,
especially _____ and _____,
will reveal Christ
through their sharing in his resurrection,
let us pray to the Lord:

\+

\+

Priest: God of all peoples,
we bring before you the gold of your
 divine life,
the incense of our prayer,
and the myrrh of our humanity.
Reveal to us the depths of your love
in the heart of our searching world;
open before us the sea of your riches;
and show us the salvation of your Son,
 Jesus Christ,
who is Lord for ever and ever. Amen.

THE BAPTISM OF THE LORD

Priest: Let us ask God's abundant blessings on us
and on all people through Jesus Christ,
with whom the Father is well pleased.

Minister: For the church,
that we live our baptismal promises as God's
　　faithful servants,
let us pray to the Lord:

For government officials,
that they be ministers of justice and peace,
let us pray to the Lord:

For all catechumens,
that they grow in their desire and love
　　for Jesus,
let us pray to the Lord:

For those facing decisions about their future,
that they come to know and accept God's will
　　for them,
let us pray to the Lord:

For those who have died,
especially _____ and _____,
that they glorify God for ever in heaven,
let us pray to the Lord:

+

+

Priest: Lord God, upholder of all,
we give you glory in company with Christ,
your beloved Son and chosen Servant.
As you gave your Holy Spirit to him,
so give your Spirit to us.
Renew in us the grace of our baptism,
so that we may serve you as beloved
    daughters and sons.
We ask this through Christ our Lord. Amen.

ASH WEDNESDAY

Priest: Let us present our needs to God,
who is gracious and merciful,
slow to anger and abounding in love.

Minister: For the church,
that it be an ambassador for Christ to
   the world
by announcing the good news
   of reconciliation,
let us pray to the Lord:

For catechumens, soon to become the elect,
that they come to true conversion
as they prepare for baptism at Easter,
let us pray to the Lord:

For those who hold public office,
that they use their authority
to safeguard the well-being and dignity of all,
let us pray to the Lord:

For all who are in agony of mind or body,
that by our friendship and help
God's love be made present to them,
let us pray to the Lord:

For ourselves,
that this Lenten season prepare us
for our passover from death to newness of life,
let us pray to the Lord:

For those who have died,
especially _____ and _____,
that they rejoice for ever in their salvation,
let us pray to the Lord:

+

+

Priest: God ever-faithful,
have mercy on your Church in its need.
As we turn away from sin,
help us turn to you in repentance.
As we leave sinfulness behind,
let us embrace your holiness with all
 our hearts.
We ask this through Christ our Lord. Amen.

FIRST SUNDAY OF LENT

Priest: In the spirit of Jesus,
who offered fervent prayer to his Father in the desert,
let us pray as God's repentant people.

Minister: That Christians everywhere may be responsive to the Word of God
during this holy season,
let us pray to the Lord:

That government leaders may work for peace
and make these days the acceptable time of God's salvation,
let us pray to the Lord:

That those who are suffering from physical illness or emotional distress
may know that God is for them in their need,
let us pray to the Lord:

That we who celebrate this Eucharist
may find strength to walk in God's ways of love and truth,
let us pray to the Lord:

That all whose journey through this life
    has ended,
especially _____ and _____,
may joyfully enter their eternal home
    in heaven,
let us pray to the Lord:

+

+

Priest: Lord God, defender of the tempted,
help your people turn again to you,
and serve you with all their hearts.
With confidence in your power over evil
we have asked your help;
may we know your mercy and love in
    our lives.
We make this prayer through Christ our Lord.
    Amen.

SECOND SUNDAY OF LENT

Priest: Let us present our needs to the Father,
who speaks to us through the beloved Son.

Minister: That the leaders of the church
will listen to the voice of God's Son
in their work for unity among Christians,
let us pray to the Lord:

That world leaders will listen to the voice of
God's Son
in their work for peace among nations,
let us pray to the Lord:

That families will listen to the voice of
God's Son
in their times of sorrow and their times of joy,
let us pray to the Lord:

That the dead,
especially _____ and _____,
will hear the voice of God's Son inviting them
to enter his kingdom,
let us pray to the Lord:

Let us listen to the voice of God's Son
as we remember our personal needs in silence.

[pause for silent prayer]

For these intentions, let us pray to the Lord:

✣

✣

Priest: Father, your favor rests on your Son, Jesus,
and on those who listen to him.
Give us the wisdom to listen to his words;
give us the strength to share in his sufferings;
give us the grace to share in his resurrection,
both now and for ever. Amen.

THIRD SUNDAY OF LENT

Priest: In company with Christ, the source of our salvation,
let us offer our fervent prayers to the God of mercy.

Minister: That all Christians will bless the Lord through their generous self-sacrifice,
let us pray to the Lord:

That those who are preparing for baptism and for reception into the Catholic Church, especially _____ and _____, will bless the Lord in faith and love,
let us pray to the Lord:

That citizens of this and every land will bless the Lord
through their pursuit of justice and peace,
let us pray to the Lord:

That our parish community will bless the Lord
through our Lenten prayer, fasting, and works of charity,
let us pray to the Lord:

That those who have died, especially _____ and _____, will bless the Lord for the divine gift of eternal life,
let us pray to the Lord:

✛

✛

Priest: Merciful and gracious God,
we ask you to receive our prayers
and answer them according to your loving-
 kindness.
Grant that our death and burial with Christ
 in baptism
may produce an abundant harvest for eternity.
We ask this through Christ our Lord. Amen.

FOURTH SUNDAY OF LENT

Priest: Together let us seek the Lord as we offer our petitions
and take refuge in the Lord's abundant mercy.

Minister: That the ministers of the church will taste the Lord's goodness
in their service to God's people,
let us pray to the Lord:

That those chosen for Christian initiation at Easter,
especially _____ and _____,
will taste the Lord's goodness
in these final weeks of preparation,
let us pray to the Lord:

That the President, the Congress, and the judiciary will taste the Lord's goodness
in their efforts for peace and justice,
let us pray to the Lord:

That the poor will taste the Lord's goodness
in our generous works of charity,
let us pray to the Lord:

That we who worship here will taste the Lord's goodness
on our journey to holy Easter,
let us pray to the Lord:

That those who have died,
especially _____ and _____,
will taste the Lord's goodness
in the gift of everlasting joy,
let us pray to the Lord:

+

+

Priest: Lord God, your Son leads us on the way
of reconciliation.
Let our prayers draw us to him in
this Eucharist,
so that we may rejoice in him now,
and live with him in your presence,
for ever and ever. Amen.

FIFTH SUNDAY OF LENT

Priest: Let us ask God to restore us and all people,
in body, soul, and spirit,
as we make our petitions.

Minister: For God's people throughout the world,
and for those who lack faith and trust in God,
let us pray to the Lord:

For those who exercise authority over others,
and for those who use violence to maintain
    their power,
let us pray to the Lord:

For those soon to be initiated and received
    into the church,
especially _____ and _____,
and for their catechists, sponsors,
    and families,
let us pray to the Lord:

For all who are weak and powerless,
especially those addicted to drugs, alcohol,
    and gambling,
let us pray to the Lord:

For us assembled here,
and for all who are seeking to know
    Christ Jesus
during these Lenten days,
let us pray to the Lord:

For the faithful departed,
especially _____ and _____,
and for all who await resurrection from
    the dead,
let us pray to the Lord:

✠

✠

Priest: Great are the wonders, Lord,
that you worked for your people Israel in
    ages past.
With them, we ask your eternal and
    merciful love,
today and every day,
both now and for ever. Amen.

PALM SUNDAY OF THE LORD'S PASSION

Priest: My sisters and brothers, as Easter draws near,
let us earnestly pray to the Lord our God.
With deep faith,
let us ask that we who are baptized,
those preparing for Christian initiation, and
the entire world,
will share more fully in the life of Christ.

Minister: That the church will become more like
Jesus Christ
in his journey through suffering to glory,
let us pray to the Lord:

That leaders of nations will become like the
Son of David in his humility,
let us pray to the Lord:

That those whose lives are poured out
in anguish
will become like the crucified Lord
in his love for others,
let us pray to the Lord:

That we who enter this Holy Week
will become like God's Suffering Servant
in his passover from death to life,
let us pray to the Lord:

That those who have died,
especially _____ and _____,
will become like their risen Savior
in his triumph over death,
let us pray to the Lord:

+

+

Priest: Merciful Father, by the death of Jesus,
 your Son,
you showed us the way to everlasting life.
Help us to accept your will for us
as obediently and confidently as he did.
Through these prayers, let us share your life
 and love,
for ever and ever. Amen.

HOLY THURSDAY

Priest: As we recall the night when Jesus gave us
a living sign of his enduring love,
let us bring our prayers before our
    gracious God.

Minister: Christ nourishes the church through
    the Eucharist.
By this sacrament, may he root our lives in
    his death
and prepare us for his coming in glory.
For this, let us pray to the Lord:

Christ spreads a table where all are nourished.
May we advance along the paths of justice
    and peace
in the strength of this food.
For this, let us pray to the Lord:

Christ's sacrifice opens us to life
in all its fullness and mystery.
May we sacrifice ourselves
for all who are starved in spirit, mind, or body.
For this, let us pray to the Lord:

Christ washed the feet of his disciples.
May we learn that the gift of salvation
binds us to serve each other in humility.
For this, let us pray to the Lord:

Christ gives us the Eucharist as the pledge of
 everlasting life.
May those who have died,
especially _____ and _____,
find lasting joy at the banquet in heaven.
For this, let us pray to the Lord:

+

+

Priest: God of love, hear the prayers we offer you
at this commemoration of your Son's life,
 death, and resurrection.
Fill us with his life through our sharing of
 this meal,
and answer our needs in your loving-
 kindness.
We ask this in the name of Jesus, our Lord
 and brother,
through whom we make our thanksgiving
 to you,
both now and for ever. Amen.

HOLY SATURDAY: EASTER VIGIL

Priest: With hearts filled with Easter joy,
let us bring our prayers to the God
who raised Jesus from the dead,
confident that the love of the Lord
is everlasting.

Minister: For the holy church of God throughout
the world,
especially its newly baptized and
received members,
especially _____ and _____,
that God's people share their Savior's triumph
over sin and death,
let us pray to the Lord:

For the rulers of nations,
that they lead us in turning oppression and
violence into justice and peace,
let us pray to the Lord:

For those who are discouraged, depressed,
or despairing,
that they find renewed hope
in the power of Jesus' resurrection,
let us pray to the Lord:

For this community of faith,
dead and risen with Christ,
that we remain grateful for the blessings
of Lent
and rejoice in the greater blessings of Easter,
let us pray to the Lord:

For those who have died,
especially _____ and _____,
that they celebrate the eternal Easter of life
    and love in God's presence,
let us pray to the Lord:

+

+

Priest: Lord God, your power is beyond compare,
and your love for us is beyond words
    to describe.
In your compassion,
answer the prayers of your ransomed people,
and grant us the riches of your mercy.
We ask this in the name of your risen Son,
    Jesus Christ,
who is Lord for ever and ever. Amen.

EASTER SUNDAY: THE RESURRECTION OF THE LORD

Priest: On this festival day,
let us present our petitions to almighty God
through Jesus Christ, our life and
our resurrection.

Minister: That the church will rejoice in
Christ's triumph
over sin and death,
let us pray to the Lord:

That those who are baptized and received into
the church this Easter,
especially _____ and _____,
will rejoice in peace from on high,
let us pray to the Lord:

That the nations of the world will rejoice in
deliverance from war
and from every threat to human life,
let us pray to the Lord:

That this assembly
will rejoice in the power flowing from
Christ's resurrection,
let us pray to the Lord:

That those who have died,
especially _____ and _____,
will rejoice for ever in glory with their
risen Savior,
let us pray to the Lord:

✚

✚

Priest: Lord God, you did not forget your beloved
 Son in death,
but raised him to life on the third day.
In his most sacred name,
we ask you to answer our prayers.
Let us share the joy of heaven,
today and every day, both now and for ever.
 Amen.

SECOND SUNDAY OF EASTER
(Divine Mercy Sunday)

Priest: Let us bring our prayers to the Father though Jesus Christ,
the glorious victor over sin and death.

Minister: That the church may be renewed in the joy of its Lord's resurrection,
let us pray to the Lord:

That the nations of the world may receive mercy in the name of Jesus Christ,
let us pray to the Lord:

That those who were baptized into Christ at Easter,
especially _____ and _____,
may rejoice in peace from on high and the salvation of their souls,
let us pray to the Lord:

That we, like Thomas,
may acclaim Jesus as our Lord and our God,
let us pray to the Lord:

That those who have died,
especially _____ and _____,
may live with their risen Savior for ever,
let us pray to the Lord:

✢

✢

Priest: **God of glory,
you raised our Lord Jesus Christ from
 the dead
and made him the joy of all believers.
Bring us to new life in Christ,
so that we may join those who now see him in
 his risen glory,
and share the blessedness of his kingdom,
both now and for ever. Amen.**

THIRD SUNDAY OF EASTER

Priest: In the saving name of Jesus,
let us offer fervent prayer for all in need.

Minister: That the Lord's power will renew the church
in the joy of Christ's resurrection,
let us pray to the Lord:

That the Lord's peace will rescue nations and
peoples from hatred and violence,
let us pray to the Lord:

That the Lord's gifts of living waters and
fertile soil
will sustain the human family,
let us pray to the Lord:

That the Lord's victory over evil will fill our
hearts with thanksgiving and praise,
let us pray to the Lord:

That the Lord's salvation will give
everlasting joy
to those who have died,
especially _____ and _____,
let us pray to the Lord:

+

+

Priest: God, our helper,
look upon us in your compassion
and grant us the riches of your kindness.
For the blessings we have received
and for those yet to come,
all honor, glory and praise are your due,
    O God,
for ever and ever. Amen.

FOURTH SUNDAY OF EASTER

Priest: Let us come before the Lord, our gladness, with these petitions.

Minister: That those who shepherd the holy church of God
will find strength in God's Word,
let us pray to the Lord:

That those who are discerning a church vocation
will find joy in God's call,
let us pray to the Lord:

That those who suffer from sickness and weakness
will find courage in God's faithfulness,
let us pray to the Lord:

That those who lack sufficient food or adequate medical care
will find assistance in God's people,
let us pray to the Lord:

That those who have died,
especially _____ and _____,
will find salvation in God's everlasting life,
let us pray to the Lord:

✢

✢

Priest: **Lord God,
we hunger and thirst for your loving-
 kindness.
Care for us well in answer to these prayers,
so that we may follow your Son to glory
and live with him in your presence,
for ever and ever. Amen.**

FIFTH SUNDAY OF EASTER

Priest: Let us pray that the salvation won by
 Jesus Christ
will bear fruit in our world
in answer to these prayers.

Minister: For ministers of the church,
that they live in Christ's love
through the strength of God,
let us pray to the Lord:

For those baptized at Easter,
especially _____ and _____,
that they live in Christ's love
through the favor of God,
let us pray to the Lord:

For those who lack food, housing,
 and employment,
that they live in Christ's love
through the generosity of God at our hands,
let us pray to the Lord:

For those who suffer from illness of mind
 or body,
especially children who are abused,
that they live in Christ's love
through the healing of God,
let us pray to the Lord:

For us who worship here,
that we live in Christ's love
through the kindness of God,
let us pray to the Lord:

For those who have died,
especially _____ and _____,
that they live for ever in Christ's love
through the mercy of God,
let us pray to the Lord:

+

+

Priest: God of love,
you have revealed your compassion to us in
    the risen Lord.
Give answer to our prayers,
so that we may love one another
as Christ has loved us,
and praise your name for ever and ever. Amen.

SIXTH SUNDAY OF EASTER

Priest: Let us bring our prayers
before the Father of Jesus Christ and
our Father.

Minister: That the members of the church,
especially those who were initiated at Easter,
will receive the power of God
in living the Christian faith,
let us pray to the Lord:

That world leaders will receive the guidance
of God
in promoting peace and justice,
let us pray to the Lord:

That parents will receive the blessing of God
in caring for their families,
let us pray to the Lord:

That those soon to graduate
will receive the goodness of God
in discovering new tasks and friends,
let us pray to the Lord:

That those who are suffering from sickness,
especially _____ and _____,
will receive the peace of God
in healing for body, mind, and spirit,
let us pray to the Lord:

That those who have died,
especially _____ and _____,
will receive the happiness of God
in living forever,
let us pray to the Lord:

+

+

Priest: We praise you, our God,
in this assembly of your people,
for your Holy Spirit
unites us to you and to your risen Son.
Answer the prayers we offer you this day,
for we make them in the name of Jesus Christ,
who is Lord for ever and ever. Amen.

ASCENSION OF THE LORD
(celebrated in some places on Sunday)

Priest: On this day when Jesus was lifted up from our midst,
let us stand before our God in solemn prayer.

Minister: That the Lord will grant wisdom and insight
to those who lead God's holy church,
let us pray to the Lord:

That the Lord will share the wealth
of the glorious heritage in Christ with all nations,
let us pray to the Lord:

That the Lord will enlighten the minds of those
who face the future with apprehension and uncertainty,
let us pray to the Lord:

That the Lord will empower the oppressed of the earth
with the strength of Christ's triumph over evil,
let us pray to the Lord:

That the Lord will raise up those who have died,
especially _____ and _____,
and grant them everlasting joy,
let us pray to the Lord:

✛

✛

Priest: Most holy God,
we ask you to answer our prayers,
so that in the time between Jesus' ascension
and his return in majesty,
we may find courage in the power of
 his blessing
and bear witness to your great love for us.
We ask this in the name of him
who has ascended to your right hand,
there to celebrate life with you and the
 Holy Spirit,
one God, for ever and ever. Amen.

SEVENTH SUNDAY OF EASTER
(where the Ascension is celebrated on Thursday)

Priest: Let us ask God to hear these petitions,
so that the life-giving water of saving grace
may be ours in abundance.

Minister: For those who lead the church,
that they proclaim God's merciful love
in their service of all,
let us pray to the Lord:

For those who govern nations and peoples,
that they reflect God's universal love
in words and works of justice,
let us pray to the Lord:

For those who suffer from poverty
    and disease,
that they know God's bountiful love
in our care and compassion,
let us pray to the Lord:

For us who worship here,
that we welcome God's abundant love in
    oneness of heart,
let us pray to the Lord:

For those who have died,
especially _____ and _____,
that they receive God's everlasting love
in the glory of heaven,
let us pray to the Lord:

\+

\+

Priest: **Lord Most High,
as Jesus, your Son, prayed for us,
so we pray for one another.
Let your love sustain us
this day and every day,
so that we will be one with you and your beloved Son,
and rejoice in you for ever and ever. Amen.**

PENTECOST

Priest: The Spirit of the Lord fills the whole world, is all-embracing, and knows the thoughts of our hearts.
In the power of the Spirit who helps us to pray rightly,
let us ask God to renew us and the face of the earth.

Minister: That the church will proclaim God's love with boldness,
let us pray to the Lord:

That nations will accept God's call to live in holiness and peace,
let us pray to the Lord:

That graduates will use God's gifts for the common good,
let us pray to the Lord:

That farmers will receive God's strength in seedtime and harvest,
let us pray to the Lord:

That the poor and the suffering
will rejoice in God's deliverance
and refreshment,
let us pray to the Lord:

That those who have died,
especially _____ and _____,
will for ever celebrate God's marvels
    accomplished in them,
let us pray to the Lord:

+

+

Priest: Father of light,
from whom every good gift comes,
send your Spirit into our lives with the power
    of a mighty wind.
Enlighten our minds by the flame of
    your wisdom;
open our hands to do your work well;
open our mouths to sing your praise,
through Jesus Christ, our Lord. Amen.

SECOND SUNDAY IN ORDINARY TIME

Priest: Let us call on the name of the Lord,
who delights in saving us and caring for us.

Minister: For the holy church of God, its ministers,
and for its renewal throughout the world,
let us pray to the Lord:

For our country, for all nations and peoples,
and for peace in every heart,
let us pray to the Lord:

For the sick, especially _____ and _____,
for those who care for them,
and for the well-being of all,
let us pray to the Lord:

For married couples, for those preparing
for marriage,
and for all that strengthens mutual love,
let us pray to the Lord:

For those who have died,
especially _____ and _____,
and for the eternal joy of the faithful departed,
let us pray to the Lord:

For those who need our prayers and whom we
now remember:

[pause for silent prayer]

For them and for ourselves,
let us pray to the Lord:

✢

✢

Priest: Lord God, our needs are great,
but your marvelous deeds for us and for
 all people
are far greater.
Hear and answer the prayers we have made to
 you this day,
for we offer them in the name of your beloved
 Son, Jesus Christ,
who is Lord for ever and ever. Amen.

THIRD SUNDAY IN ORDINARY TIME

Priest: Let us ask to know the Lord's kindness
 and faithfulness
in answer to these prayers.

Minister: For the unity of the holy church of God
and for the well-being of the human family,
let us pray to the Lord:

For the building of a more humane world
and for respect for all human life,
let us pray to the Lord:

For the elimination of disease, famine,
 and war,
and for the reconciliation of states
 and peoples,
let us pray to the Lord:

For the recovery of the sick,
especially _____ and _____,
and for the deliverance of the oppressed,
let us pray to the Lord:

For the consolation of the dying,
and for the eternal happiness of those who
 have died,
especially _____ and _____,
let us pray to the Lord:

        +

        +

Priest: **Lord, let the words of our prayers and the thoughts of our hearts
find favor in your sight,
so that rejoicing in your saving power may be our strength.
We ask this through Christ our Lord. Amen.**

FOURTH SUNDAY IN ORDINARY TIME

Priest: Let us call upon our God, who sustains us in good times and bad.

Minister: For the church,
that its ministers and people reveal the reign of God in this world,
let us pray to the Lord:

For all nations, peoples and communities,
that they accept God's call to live in holiness and peace,
let us pray to the Lord:

For the poor and the oppressed,
that their cries for justice be quickly answered,
let us pray to the Lord:

For ourselves,
that we be strong in faith and generous in love,
let us pray to the Lord:

For those who have died,
especially _____ and _____,
that they receive the joys of everlasting life,
let us pray to the Lord:

\+

\+

Priest: God of love, our refuge and strength,
we ask you to answer these prayers.
Be for us a helper close at hand in all
 our needs.
We ask this in the name of Jesus the Lord.
 Amen.

FIFTH SUNDAY IN ORDINARY TIME

Priest: In the sight of the angels,
let us call upon the name of the Lord
and ask to receive God's everlasting love.

Minister: That God's holiness
will sanctify all servants of the Gospel,
let us pray to the Lord:

That God's truth
will guide public officials in every land,
let us pray to the Lord:

That God's deliverance
will console the hungry and the homeless,
let us pray to the Lord:

That God's healing
will save the sick and the injured,
especially _____ and _____,
let us pray to the Lord:

That God's strength
will empower those with disabilities,
let us pray to the Lord:

That God's kindness
will lead us to give thanks to the Lord in
 this Eucharist,
let us pray to the Lord:

That God's salvation
will become the praise of those who
 have died,
especially _____ and _____,
let us pray to the Lord:

+

+

Priest: Great is your glory, Lord,
in making us followers of your Son,
 Jesus Christ.
Grant us what we need
to complete your work in us and through us.
We ask this through the same Christ our Lord.
 Amen.

SIXTH SUNDAY IN ORDINARY TIME

Priest: Let us place our trust in the Lord,
who is eager to give us what we ask in
these prayers.

Minister: That the church will know God's blessing
in preaching the Gospel of the risen Christ,
let us pray to the Lord:

That the United Nations and
international organizations
will know God's blessing
in their efforts for peace and justice,
let us pray to the Lord:

That wives and husbands will know God's
blessing
in their mutual love,
let us pray to the Lord:

That the sick will know God's blessing
in restored health and wholeness,
let us pray to the Lord:

That those who lack food, shelter,
and clothing
will know God's blessing in our
abundant generosity,
let us pray to the Lord:

That those who have died,
especially _____ and _____,
will know God's blessing in eternal life,
let us pray to the Lord:

+

+

Priest: Lord, we ask you to answer these prayers.
As you turn your heart to us in blessing,
turn our hearts to you in hope and love.
We ask this through Christ our Lord. Amen.

SEVENTH SUNDAY IN ORDINARY TIME

Priest: The Lord pardons our iniquities and heals our ills.
Let us ask to become God's pardon and healing for others
in these petitions.

Minister: For divine and human goodness in all believers,
let us pray to the Lord:

For divine and human compassion in all who govern,
let us pray to the Lord:

For divine and human compassion toward victims of famine, disease, and violence,
let us pray to the Lord:

For divine and human mercy in every heart,
let us pray to the Lord:

For divine and human remembrance of those who have died,
especially _____ and _____,
let us pray to the Lord:

✛

✛

Priest: Lord God, your gifts to us are overflowing.
Answer our prayers,
so that your abundant generosity to us
will become our gift to others in your name.
We ask this through Christ our Lord. Amen.

EIGHTH SUNDAY IN ORDINARY TIME

Priest: Out of the divine goodness that grows in our hearts
through the Holy Spirit,
let us pray for our needs and the needs of all people.

Minister: That those who guide the mission of the church
may be selfless in preaching the Gospel of Jesus Christ,
let us pray to the Lord:

That world leaders and government officials
may be steadfast in building up the human family,
let us pray to the Lord:

That all people in their own vocation
may be fully devoted to the Lord's work,
let us pray to the Lord:

That we who sing songs of praise in this assembly
may be generous in serving the needy outside it,
let us pray to the Lord:

That those who have died, especially
 _____ and _____,
may be clothed in the immortality won by
 Christ's victory over death,
let us pray to the Lord:

+

+

Priest: God of saints and sinners,
as we open our ears to hear your Son's Word,
we ask you to open our lives
to receive what is for our good
in answer to these prayers.
Yours be the praise and the glory,
now and always, through Jesus Christ, our
 Lord. Amen.

NINTH SUNDAY IN ORDINARY TIME

Priest: Gathered in this holy house,
let us confidently call upon our God
in these prayers.

Minister: That all who serve the church may know God's strength
in the grace of Jesus Christ,
let us pray to the Lord:

That nations and peoples may know God's kindness
in the peace of Jesus Christ,
let us pray to the Lord:

That those who suffer in body, mind, or spirit
may know God's salvation
in the compassion of Jesus Christ,
let us pray to the Lord:

That we may know God's fidelity
in the love of Jesus Christ,
let us pray to the Lord:

That those who have died,
especially _____ and _____,
may know God's mercy
in the resurrection of Jesus Christ,
let us pray to the Lord:

✢

✢

Priest: God of every nation,
with the faith-filled centurion in the gospel
we trust in your Son's power
to help and save us.
Answer our prayers as we call out to you in
 his name,
Jesus Christ, our Lord. Amen.

TENTH SUNDAY IN ORDINARY TIME

Priest: God has called us to be a holy people
through the Gospel of Jesus Christ.
In his most sacred name,
let us ask God to hear our prayers.

Minister: For God's gift of new life
to empower the ministers of this parish
and of the church throughout the world,
let us pray to the Lord:

For God's gift of new life
to rescue all people from poverty, injustice,
and war,
let us pray to the Lord:

For God's gift of new life
to heal those who suffer from illness and
injury,
let us pray to the Lord:

For God's gift of new life
to renew and refresh all who worship here,
let us pray to the Lord:

For God's gift of new and everlasting life
to deliver those who have died,
especially _____ and _____,
let us pray to the Lord:

+

+

Priest: God of the living,
you come to meet us in every need.
By your gift of new life,
turn our fervent petitions into thankful praise,
through Jesus Christ, our Lord. Amen.

ELEVENTH SUNDAY IN ORDINARY TIME

Priest: Jesus Christ loved us and gave himself up for us,
so that we might be put right with God.
Let us pray for our needs and the needs of people everywhere.

Minister: That the leaders of the church will live for God
by seeking the unity of all Christians,
let us pray to the Lord:

That the nations and peoples of the earth
will live for God
by embracing justice and peace,
let us pray to the Lord:

That fathers and mothers will live for God
by generously serving their families in love,
let us pray to the Lord:

That those oppressed by any need
will live for God
by believing firmly in Jesus Christ,
let us pray to the Lord:

That we who worship here will live for God
by forgiving each other from our hearts,
let us pray to the Lord:

That all who have died,
especially _____ and _____,
will live for God
by sharing in Christ's resurrection,
let us pray to the Lord:

+

+

Priest: Lord, though we are sinners,
you have taken away our guilt.
Shelter us and all people in answer to
    our prayers,
so that we may rejoice in you,
both now and for ever. Amen.

TWELFTH SUNDAY IN ORDINARY TIME

Priest: My sisters and brothers,
God has poured out a spirit of grace and
 petition upon us,
and so we ask God to hear our prayers.

Minister: For the leaders of the church,
clothed with Christ in their service to all,
let us pray to the Lord:

For leaders of nations,
clothed with Christ in their care for their
 people,
let us pray to the Lord:

For the hungry, homeless, and unemployed,
clothed with Christ in their sufferings,
let us pray to the Lord:

For ourselves,
clothed with Christ in our call to discipleship,
let us pray to the Lord:

For those who have died,
especially _____ and _____,
clothed with Christ in the promise of his
 resurrection,
let us pray to the Lord:

+

+

Priest: Almighty God, you have made us one in
 Christ Jesus.
In his name, we ask you to share with us
and with all your people the blessings of our
 inheritance in Christ,
this day and every day,
both now and for ever. Amen.

THIRTEENTH SUNDAY IN ORDINARY TIME

Priest: Having heard the words of everlasting life, let us bring our needs to God in this common prayer.

Minister: For the ministers of the church, that they experience the joy of generous service for the reign of God, let us pray to the Lord:

For public officials, that they achieve success in their efforts to build up the human family, let us pray to the Lord:

For the people of all nations, that they know the blessings of prosperity, harmony, and justice, let us pray to the Lord:

For all who travel and vacation during this season, that they enjoy safety and refreshment in their leisure time, let us pray to the Lord:

For us who celebrate the Eucharist in this place, that we find renewed strength in following the Lord Jesus, let us pray to the Lord:

For those who have died,
especially _____ and _____,
that they know delight at God's right hand
    for ever,
let us pray to the Lord:

+

+

Priest: Lord God, you have set us on the way
    of discipleship.
As we journey together,
we ask you to answer our prayers.
Grant that your Son be for us and for
    all people
our joyful inheritance,
this day and every day, both now and for ever.
    Amen.

FOURTEENTH SUNDAY IN ORDINARY TIME

Priest: Let us ask peace and mercy for all in need, both in this community and throughout all the earth.

Minister: That Christians will know the Lord's power
in living as a new creation,
let us pray to the Lord:

That nations and peoples will know the
    Lord's power
in all that leads to peace and justice,
let us pray to the Lord:

That the poor and the oppressed
will know the Lord's power
in their deliverance from suffering,
let us pray to the Lord:

That we who follow the rule of life in
    Christ Jesus
will know the Lord's power in this Eucharist,
let us pray to the Lord:

That those who have died,
especially _____ and _____,
will know the Lord's power in fullness of joy,
let us pray to the Lord:

✢

✢

Priest: **Comforting God,**
refuse not our prayers,
so that our hearts may rejoice
in your mighty works.
We ask this through Christ our Lord. Amen.

FIFTEENTH SUNDAY IN ORDINARY TIME

Priest: Let us turn to the Lord with fervent prayer, asking that the Lord's voice will renew in us our love for God and neighbor.

Minister: For the leaders of the churches,
that they will heed the Lord's voice
calling Christians to unity,
let us pray to the Lord:

For those who seek solutions to global
 economic problems,
that they will obey the Lord's voice
calling them to promote justice and peace,
let us pray to the Lord:

For those who suffer from illness
 and violence,
that they will hear the Lord's voice
calling them to wholeness,
let us pray to the Lord:

For us who celebrate the Eucharist this day,
that we will respond to the Lord's voice
calling us to mutual love,
let us pray to the Lord:

For those who have died,
especially _____ and _____,
that they will rejoice in the Lord's voice
calling them to everlasting life,
let us pray to the Lord:

✢

✢

Priest: Gracious and merciful God,
you have given us the fullness of your love in
 Christ Jesus.
May the words of our mouths,
the thoughts of our hearts,
and the work of our hands,
proclaim the holiness we find in your
 beloved Son.
Help us live as members of his Body,
one with you and with each other
in the bond of love,
both now and for ever. Amen.

SIXTEENTH SUNDAY IN ORDINARY TIME

Priest: Let us bring our needs to the God of glory,
who has come close to us in Jesus Christ.

Minister: That all who serve the community of believers
will live in the Lord's presence
through their ministry,
let us pray to the Lord:

That nations and peoples will live in the
    Lord's presence
through their commitment to peace,
let us pray to the Lord:

That those who suffer from neglect and abuse
will live in the Lord's presence
through our words and deeds of compassion,
let us pray to the Lord:

That we will live in the Lord's presence
through God's gifts to us in this Eucharist,
let us pray to the Lord:

That those who have died,
especially _____ and _____,
will live in the Lord's presence
through sharing Christ's resurrection,
let us pray to the Lord:

+

+

Priest: Lord, with Mary of Bethany
we open wide our ears to hear your word;
with Martha, we open wide our hands to do
   your work.
Let our prayers today
center our lives on your Son, Jesus Christ,
who is Lord for ever and ever. Amen.

SEVENTEENTH SUNDAY IN ORDINARY TIME

Priest: Let us call upon God our Savior in fervent prayer.

Minister: That the all-powerful God
will be the church's power for good,
let us pray to the Lord:

That the all-reconciling God
will be the reconciliation of states
 and peoples,
let us pray to the Lord:

That the all-saving God
will be the salvation of the sick and the poor,
the hungry and the homeless,
let us pray to the Lord:

That the all-protecting God
will be the protection of all who defend us,
especially police officers and firefighters,
let us pray to the Lord:

That the all-strong God
will be the strength of this parish community,
let us pray to the Lord:

That the all-merciful God
will be the mercy of those who have died,
especially _____ and _____,
let us pray to the Lord:

✛

✛

Priest: **Generous God,**
as Jesus taught us, we knock on the door of
**   your mercy,**
and seek your good gifts for body, soul,
**   and spirit.**
Give us what you have inspired us
to ask of you in faith,
through Jesus Christ, our Lord. Amen.

EIGHTEENTH SUNDAY IN ORDINARY TIME

Priest: With great confidence,
let us ask the Lord's kindness and faithfulness
for us and for all God's servants.

Minister: For the welfare of the holy church of God
and for the well-being of the human family,
let us pray to the Lord:

For the elimination of disease, famine,
　and war,
and for an end to hatred and violence,
especially in the Middle East and in Africa,
let us pray to the Lord:

For the recovery of the sick
and for the deliverance of the oppressed,
let us pray to the Lord:

For seasonable weather, sufficient rainfall, and
　bountiful harvests,
and for a just return for human labor,
let us pray to the Lord:

For the consolation of the dying
and for the eternal happiness of those who
　have died,
especially _____ and _____,
let us pray to the Lord:

        ✢

        ✢

Priest: **Father,**
we rejoice in your never-failing help.
Show us the greatness of your love,
and answer our prayers in your great mercy.
We ask this through Christ our Lord. Amen.

NINETEENTH SUNDAY IN ORDINARY TIME

Priest: As the people the Lord has blessed in Christ Jesus,
let us ask God's blessing on us and on our world
in these prayers.

Minister: That the Lord's kindness
will be upon the members of the church
and be their source of faith,
let us pray to the Lord:

That the Lord's kindness
will be upon all peoples of the earth
and be their deliverance from every danger,
let us pray to the Lord:

That the Lord's kindness
will be upon those weakened by mental and physical suffering,
especially _____ and _____,
and be their comfort in distress,
let us pray to the Lord:

That the Lord's kindness
will be upon us who worship here
and be our help in every need,
let us pray to the Lord:

That the Lord's kindness
will be upon all who have died,
especially _____ and _____,
and be their peace for ever,
let us pray to the Lord:

✢

✢

Priest: Increase our faith, ever-faithful God,
so that with your holy ones of old
we may embrace your kindness in our lives
and share it with others
according to your will.
We ask this through Christ our Lord. Amen.

TWENTIETH SUNDAY IN ORDINARY TIME

Priest: Faith is God's gift to those who doubt,
courage to those who are afraid,
and strength to those who are weak.
Let us ask God to hear these petitions.

Minister: That the church will receive the power
of Jesus
in its witness to his Gospel,
let us pray to the Lord:

That public officials will receive the strength
of Jesus
in their defense of human rights,
let us pray to the Lord:

That the young and the aged, the poor and
the suffering,
will receive the consolation of Jesus in
their need,
let us pray to the Lord:

That we who celebrate this Eucharist
will receive the perseverance of Jesus
in our life of faith,
let us pray to the Lord:

That those who kept their eyes fixed on Jesus
in this life,
especially _____ and _____,
will receive the vision of Jesus in heaven,
let us pray to the Lord:

+

+

Priest: **Father,
trusting in your goodness
we ask you to answer our prayers.
Come to our aid, come to our aid,
so that the living flame of love
in the heart of Jesus and in our hearts
will brighten our world.
We ask this through Christ our Lord. Amen.**

TWENTY-FIRST SUNDAY IN ORDINARY TIME

Priest: With trust in God as wide as our need,
let us offer these petitions.

Minister: For the community of believers in this and
every place,
and for those who witness to God's love for
all peoples,
let us pray to the Lord:

For the children of God throughout the earth,
especially those forced to live less than the
life for which God made them,
let us pray to the Lord:

For the poor and the ill,
in our midst and far away,
and for those who care for their needs
in humility,
let us pray to the Lord:

For us who know the kindness and fidelity of
the Lord in our worship,
and for those who have strayed from
Christ's church,
let us pray to the Lord:

For those who have been called
to God's kingdom in death,
especially _____ and _____,
and for those who mourn them,
let us pray to the Lord:

+

+

Priest: God of holiness, as you receive our prayers,
welcome us to your table with all your
    holy ones.
Let us share your feast of life and love,
both now and for ever. Amen.

TWENTY-SECOND SUNDAY IN ORDINARY TIME

Priest: How great is the mercy of the Lord!
God's loving-kindness is everlasting!
Let us pray for the church, the world,
and for people everywhere.

Minister: That God's goodness will provide
more vocations
for the church's mission,
let us pray to the Lord:

That God's goodness will provide
abundant help
for all who suffer in body or spirit,
especially _____ and _____,
let us pray to the Lord:

That God's goodness will provide sure hope
for those who have lost their way,
let us pray to the Lord:

That God's goodness will provide
generous gifts
for this assembly of worshipers,
let us pray to the Lord:

That God's goodness will provide an
everlasting home
for all who have died,
especially _____ and _____,
let us pray to the Lord:

+

+

Priest: **Gracious God,
let your infinite goodness be ours
in answer to these prayers,
for we make them in the name of your
beloved Son,
Jesus Christ, who is Lord for ever and ever.
Amen.**

TWENTY-THIRD SUNDAY IN ORDINARY TIME

Priest: Let us call upon the Lord, our refuge in every age,
and offer fervent prayer for all in need.

Minister: That the Lord's gracious care
will sustain the church in its witness to the Gospel,
let us pray to the Lord:

That the Lord's gracious care
will protect the rulers of nations and their people,
let us pray to the Lord:

That the Lord's gracious care
will deliver the poor and the oppressed from suffering,
let us pray to the Lord:

That the Lord's gracious care
will help us to know God's will and to do it,
let us pray to the Lord:

That the Lord's gracious care
will become everlasting life and joy
for those who have died,
especially _____ and _____,
let us pray to the Lord:

✢

✢

Priest: **Lord,
your Holy Spirit guides us on the path
   of discipleship.
By our prayers,
renew the power of that Spirit in every heart,
so that we may judge wisely the things
   of earth
and love the things of heaven.
We ask this through Christ our Lord. Amen.**

TWENTY-FOURTH SUNDAY IN ORDINARY TIME

Priest: My sisters and brothers,
let us pray that the grace of Jesus Christ
will be abundant for us and for all people
in need.

Minister: For those who teach the Christian faith
in our parish, in our diocese and throughout
the world,
let us pray to the Lord:

For those who promote justice and peace in
this and every land,
let us pray to the Lord:

For those who suffer from poverty
and sickness,
especially _____ and _____,
let us pray to the Lord:

For us who proclaim the Lord's praise in
this Eucharist,
let us pray to the Lord:

For those who have died in the hope of
everlasting life,
especially _____ and _____,
let us pray to the Lord:

✛

✛

Priest: Great is your compassion, O Lord,
toward us and all your people.
Let your goodness be seen in answer to
our prayers.
Honor and glory be yours in Christ Jesus,
both now and for ever. Amen.

TWENTY-FIFTH SUNDAY IN ORDINARY TIME

Priest: The Lord Jesus presents our needs to God
and protects those who dwell in him.
Let us ask him to unite us in his peace
as we pray in his name.

Minister: That leaders of the church
will receive the Lord's guidance in
    their ministry,
let us pray to the Lord:

That leaders of governments and those
    in authority
will imitate the Lord's love for justice
in their words and deeds,
let us pray to the Lord:

That victims of domestic and gang violence
will enjoy the Lord's healing in their need,
let us pray to the Lord:

That we who worship here
will live in the power of the Lord's truth,
let us pray to the Lord:

That those who have died,
especially _____ and _____,
will rejoice in the Lord's salvation in heaven,
let us pray to the Lord:

Let us remember our particular needs.

    [pause for silent prayer]

For these needs, let us pray to the Lord:

✢

✢

Priest: Lord God, maker of heaven and earth,
we raise our hands and hearts to you in
 fervent prayer.
In your love, guard us from every danger
and grant us your salvation.
We ask this through Christ our Lord. Amen.

TWENTY-SIXTH SUNDAY IN ORDINARY TIME

Priest: With confidence in God's love and mercy,
let us present our needs to the Lord.

Minister: For Pope _____, (Arch) Bishop
_____,
and all who serve the church,
that God's strength be theirs
as they witness to Jesus Christ,
let us pray to the Lord:

For leaders of governments,
that God's protection be theirs
as they work for justice and peace,
let us pray to the Lord:

For the poor, the hungry and the homeless,
the sick and the injured,
that God's deliverance be theirs
as they receive our words of hope and deeds
    of love,
let us pray to the Lord:

For those who have died,
especially _____ and _____,
that God's joy be theirs
as they celebrate eternal life,
let us pray to the Lord:

Let us remember our particular intentions.

[pause for silent prayer]

That God's help be ours in every need,
let us pray to the Lord:

+

+

Priest: God of all consolation,
hear our prayers for your good gifts.
Help us to live as unselfishly
as did your Son, Jesus Christ,
and so come to live with him in your presence,
for ever and ever. Amen.

TWENTY-SEVENTH SUNDAY IN ORDINARY TIME

Priest: With faith in Christ Jesus, who gives us life in abundance,
let us pray for the needs of all God's children.

Minister: For the church's proclamation and promotion of every effort to establish God's peace throughout the world,
let us pray to the Lord:

For an opening of every heart to those who lack the necessities of human life,
let us pray to the Lord:

For wisdom to recognize and reverence every person
as God's gift, especially the unborn, the elderly, the terminally ill and the desperately poor,
let us pray to the Lord:

For the strengthening of all who are afflicted in body, mind, and spirit,
let us pray to the Lord:

For fullness of life in God's presence for all who have died,
especially _____ and _____,
let us pray to the Lord:

\+

\+

Priest: Gracious God, source of all life,
you have called us by name
and made us your people.
We ask a full portion of your goodness
in every human heart.
Let our faith and love establish our lives
 in peace,
for the life of the world.
We ask this through Christ our Lord. Amen.

TWENTY-EIGHTH SUNDAY IN ORDINARY TIME

Priest: Let us pray for all in need,
here in our midst and throughout all the earth.

Minister: That Christians will know the Lord's
saving power
in the Word of God and the sacraments,
let us pray to the Lord:

That nations and peoples will know the Lord's
saving power
in all that leads to justice and peace,
let us pray to the Lord:

That the sick and the poor will know the
Lord's saving power
in their deliverance from suffering,
let us pray to the Lord:

That we who seek to live with Christ
will know the Lord's saving power in
this Eucharist,
let us pray to the Lord:

That those who have died,
especially _____ and _____,
will know the Lord's saving power
in reigning with Christ,
let us pray to the Lord:

Let us ask the Lord's saving power as we remember our particular needs.

[pause for silent prayer]

For all our needs, let us pray to the Lord:

+

+

Priest: Lord our God,
how tremendous are your deeds, how marvelous your works!
Answer our prayers,
for with the grateful leper in the gospel,
we trust in your Son's power
to help and save us.
With Naaman we say:
Yours be the praise and the glory, for ever and ever! Amen.

TWENTY-NINTH SUNDAY IN ORDINARY TIME

Priest: Our help in every need is from the Lord.
In company with Christ, let us offer
  these petitions
to the God who upholds our lives.

Minister: That missionaries at home and abroad
will receive the Lord's protection
as they preach the Word of God,
let us pray to the Lord:

That leaders of governments
will imitate the Lord's love for justice
in their words and deeds,
let us pray to the Lord:

That the sick, especially _____ and
_____,
will enjoy the Lord's healing and comfort,
let us pray to the Lord:

That we will welcome the Lord's
  saving wisdom
in the Scriptures that enliven our prayer
  and work,
let us pray to the Lord:

That those who have died,
especially _____ and _____,
will rejoice in the Lord's salvation for ever,
let us pray to the Lord:

+

+

Priest: God our strength, we turn to you.
Show us your great love
in answer to these prayers,
and hear those who call out to you
day and night, in every place.
We ask this through Christ our Lord. Amen.

THIRTIETH SUNDAY IN ORDINARY TIME

Priest: Let us call upon the Lord,
who is always close to those who seek mercy.

Minister: For the holy church of God,
that it will have unity and peace throughout
the world,
let us pray to the Lord:

For civil authorities,
that God will direct their hearts and minds for
our well-being,
let us pray to the Lord:

For the sick, the hungry, and the homeless,
that God working through us
will speedily answer their cries for help,
let us pray to the Lord:

For this assembly of God's people,
that we will grow in the humility of
Jesus Christ,
let us pray to the Lord:

For all who have died,
especially _____ and _____,
that they will celebrate Christ's victory over
sin and death
in his heavenly kingdom,
let us pray to the Lord:

Let us remember our particular needs.

[pause for silent prayer]

For these needs, let us pray to the Lord:

+

+

Priest: **Lord our God,**
your mercy toward the humble
    is measureless,
and your love is beyond words to describe.
Look upon us in your great kindness,
and grant us the riches of your favor,
through Jesus Christ, our Lord. Amen.

THIRTY-FIRST SUNDAY IN ORDINARY TIME

Priest: Because Jesus delights in seeking us and saving us,
let us confidently present our needs to the God of mercy in his name.

Minister: For our Holy Father, our bishop, our pastor, and the staff of this parish,
let us pray to the Lord:

For the members of this community of faith, and for those preparing to become members,
let us pray to the Lord:

For our national, state, and local officials,
let us pray to the Lord:

For the unemployed, the hungry, and the homeless,
and for those who are ill or injured,
especially _____ and _____,
let us pray to the Lord:

For those who are lost
in the darkness of addiction to alcohol, drugs, and gambling,
let us pray to the Lord:

For the faithful departed,
especially _____ and _____,
let us pray to the Lord:

✢

✢

Priest: **Lord God,
our need for your mercy is great,
but your love for us and for all people is far greater.
Hear and answer the prayers we present to you this day,
for we make them in the name of your beloved Son, Jesus Christ,
who is Lord for ever and ever. Amen.**

THIRTY-SECOND SUNDAY IN ORDINARY TIME

Priest: Let us call upon the Lord,
who is near to us both in life and in death.

Minister: That the Lord's strength
will empower all believers
for every good deed and word,
let us pray to the Lord:

That the Lord's guidance
will direct our public servants
along the paths of justice and peace,
let us pray to the Lord:

That the Lord's protection
will shield all military personnel from danger,
let us pray to the Lord:

That the Lord's salvation
will speedily deliver the people of this and
    every country
from poverty, hunger, and homelessness,
let us pray to the Lord:

That the Lord's consolation
will comfort the sick and the dying,
let us pray to the Lord:

That the Lord's mercy
will embrace those who have died,
especially those killed in warfare,
and also _____ and _____,
let us pray to the Lord:

✠

✠

Priest: **God our Savior,
your kindness extends to all people
and your faithfulness knows no limits.
Answer our prayers for the sake of him
whose death won our everlasting life,
your Son, Jesus Christ,
who lives and reigns for ever and ever. Amen.**

THIRTY-THIRD SUNDAY IN ORDINARY TIME

Priest: Let us present our prayers to the Lord,
who has come to rule the earth in Jesus Christ

Minister: That the members of the church
will receive renewed strength in God's love,
let us pray to the Lord:

That all nations and peoples
will find lasting peace
in God's plan for this world,
let us pray to the Lord:

That the ill and infirm
will enjoy abundant comfort in God's healing,
let us pray to the Lord:

That all who worship here
will place sure confidence in God's salvation,
let us pray to the Lord:

That the dying and those who have died,
especially _____ and _____,
will know eternal joy in God's reign,
let us pray to the Lord:

✢

✢

Priest: **All-holy God,**
let your sun of righteousness, our Lord
**   Jesus Christ,**
rise in our hearts and brighten our days.
Draw us to him in this Eucharist,
so that we may welcome him now,
and live with him in your presence,
for ever and ever. Amen.

OUR LORD JESUS CHRIST THE KING

Priest: In union with Christ our King,
let us ask God to hear and answer our prayers.

Minister: That the members of Christ's Body
will become like their Head
in his suffering and in his glory,
let us pray to the Lord:

That leaders of nations
will become like the Son of David
in his humility,
let us pray to the Lord:

That those who are poured out in anguish,
especially those living with HIV and AIDS,
will become like God's Suffering Servant
in his fullness of life,
let us pray to the Lord:

That those who are captives to self-love
will become like the crucified Lord
in his love for others,
let us pray to the Lord:

That those who have died,
especially _____ and _____,
will become like their risen Savior
in his triumph over death,
let us pray to the Lord:

+

+

Priest: Almighty and eternal God,
you willed to reconcile all things in your
    beloved Son,
the King and center of our hearts.
Help us to live the truth of his kingship,
so that we may share the lot of the saints
    in light.
Accompany us on the way to your house,
and, at journey's end,
give us everlasting joy in your kingdom.
We ask this through Christ our Lord. Amen.

THE MOST HOLY TRINITY

Priest: God's Holy Spirit now leads us into prayer
and gives us the assurance that God will hear
our petitions.

Minister: For the Christian churches,
that they be one in the unifying love of the
Father, Son and Holy Spirit,
let us pray to the Lord:

For civil authorities,
that they intensify their efforts
to establish peace and justice throughout
the world,
let us pray to the Lord:

For the homeless and the hungry, the sick and
the dying,
that they receive consolation from the God
who saves,
let us pray to the Lord:

For all who have gathered here,
that we welcome the love of God,
poured into our hearts in this Eucharist,
let us pray to the Lord:

For those who have died,
especially _____ and _____,
that they share the glory of the Triune God,
let us pray to the Lord:

✢

✢

Priest: Lord God, have mercy on us and answer
 our prayers.
Let the love which unites the Persons of
 the Trinity
shape our lives and the lives of all people.
We ask this in the name of Jesus, your Son,
who celebrates life with you and the
 Holy Spirit,
one God, for ever and ever. Amen.

THE MOST HOLY BODY AND BLOOD OF CHRIST

Priest: Let us ask our generous God to be mindful of us in our need.

Minister: That those who lead the churches
will help us live as the one Body of Christ,
let us pray to the Lord:

That national and local agencies
will satisfy the human hunger for peace
    and justice,
let us pray to the Lord:

That those who suffer in body, mind, and spirit
will be gladdened by many signs
of divine and human love for them,
let us pray to the Lord:

That this assembly
will delight in Christ's gift of himself in
    the Eucharist,
let us pray to the Lord:

That the dead,
especially _____ and _____,
will be raised up to sing God's praise
    in heaven,
let us pray to the Lord:

✢

✢

Priest: Nourishing God,
nothing is lacking to those who love you.
Multiply your blessings among us
for our good and your glory.
Yours be the praise and the glory
through Jesus Christ, for ever and ever. Amen.

THE MOST SACRED HEART OF JESUS

Priest: As we honor the Most Sacred Heart of Jesus,
formed by the Holy Spirit in the womb of the
Virgin Mother,
let us present our needs to almighty God.

Minister: That Jesus, fountain of life and holiness,
will keep the church holy and pure
in its witness to the Gospel,
let us pray to the Lord:

That Jesus, ruler and center of all hearts,
will lead the nations in the ways of peace,
let us pray to the Lord:

That Jesus, source of all consolation,
will give comfort to the sick and the dying,
especially _____ and _____,
let us pray to the Lord:

That Jesus, salvation of those who trust
in him,
will draw us to himself
in his saving death and resurrection,
let us pray to the Lord:

That Jesus, hope of those who die in him,
will raise up all the faithful departed,
especially _____ and _____,
let us pray to the Lord:

✣

✣

Priest: God of mercy,
your beloved Son accepted death on a cross
   for us.
Receive our prayers for the sake of him
whose heart was filled with your infinite love.
We ask this through our Good Shepherd,
   Jesus Christ,
who is Lord for ever and ever. Amen.

December 8

THE IMMACULATE CONCEPTION OF THE BLESSED VIRGIN MARY

Priest: In company with the sinless Mother of God,
patroness of the United States,
let us ask God to look upon us with favor,
and to hear the prayers we offer
for the entire human family.

Minister: For the ministers of the church,
that they preach the message of salvation with
Mary's humility,
let us pray to the Lord:

For civil leaders and the citizens of all nations,
that they establish peace and justice with
Mary's integrity,
let us pray to the Lord:

For all who suffer from illness or hardship,
that they trust in the surpassing love of God
with Mary's perseverance,
let us pray to the Lord:

For parents and their children,
that they serve each other's needs with
Mary's generosity,
let us pray to the Lord:

For this assembly,
that we praise God's glory with
Mary's reverence,
let us pray to the Lord:

> For those who have died,
> especially _____ and _____,
> that they celebrate around God's throne with
>   Mary's joy,
> let us pray to the Lord:
>
> +
>
> +

Priest: **Praise to you, God and Father of our Lord
    Jesus Christ,
for hearing our prayers in your great mercy,
and for bestowing on us
every spiritual blessing for our salvation.
Grant that we, like Mary,
will share abundantly in the holiness of
    your Son,
and praise the divine grace you have given us
    in him,
for ever and ever. Amen.**

December 12

OUR LADY OF GUADALUPE
(United States of America)

Priest: The God of glory honored the Blessed Virgin Mary
by changing Tepeyac's barren ground
into a fragrant garden of flowers.
Let us ask God
to transform the rough places of our hearts and of our world,
so that our lives may bear the imprint of Mary's virtues.

Minister: That the all-holy God be the holiness
of those called to share the life of God's Son,
the Savior of all nations,
let us pray to the Lord:

That the all-powerful God be the power
of all who serve in the ordained ministry and in the religious life,
let us pray to the Lord:

That the all-saving God be the salvation
of those oppressed by poverty and injustice throughout the earth,
let us pray to the Lord:

That the all-protecting God be the protection
of the Americas
through the intercession of Our Lady of Guadalupe, our patroness,
let us pray to the Lord:

That the all-merciful God be the mercy of
 those who have died,
especially _____ and _____,
let us pray to the Lord:

+

+

Priest: Almighty and everlasting God,
you willed that your Word should take flesh
in the womb of the Blessed Virgin Mary.
Grant that we who honor her as Our Lady
 of Guadalupe
may be delivered by her prayers
from all sin and sorrow,
and may be welcomed to the joys of our
 heavenly home.
We ask this through Christ our Lord. Amen.

January (third Monday)

MARTIN LUTHER KING, JR., HOLIDAY
(United States of America)

Priest: Blessed be our God
for making peace the fruit of justice and love.
As we honor the memory of Reverend Doctor
Martin Luther King Jr.,
let us ask God to direct our lives
to bring forth this fruit in harmony.

Minister: That the church will be united and preserved
in the bonds of peace,
let us pray to the Lord:

That civic leaders will promote mutual
understanding and respect
between different ethnic groups
in our area and throughout the world,
let us pray to the Lord:

That the children of God will enrich
each other
through their diversity and common goals,
let us pray to the Lord:

That all who suffer from prejudice
and poverty
will find deliverance in renewed zeal for
justice throughout our land,
let us pray to the Lord:

That we will rid our hearts of the fear
and jealousy
that threaten peace in our midst,
let us pray to the Lord:

That those who have died,
especially those martyred in the struggle for
 civil rights,
will live for ever with the God of glory,
let us pray to the Lord:

+

+

Priest: Lord God, creator of the human family,
your Son reconciles us to you and to
 each other.
Answer our prayers in your mercy,
so that the power of Jesus Christ, working
 in us,
will bring all people together in mutual love.
We ask this through the same Christ our Lord.
 Amen.

March 19

ST. JOSEPH, HUSBAND OF THE BLESSED VIRGIN MARY

Priest: In company with Saint Joseph, head of the Holy Family,
let us ask God's blessing upon the human family in these prayers.

Minister: With Joseph most strong, we ask protection for the holy church of God throughout the world.
For this we pray:

With Joseph most prudent, we ask for right judgment
in all who govern.
For this we pray:

With Joseph most just, we ask justice
for oppressed workers of the earth.
For this we pray:

With Joseph most obedient,
we ask for hearts ready to do God's work.
For this we pray:

With Joseph most faithful, we ask God's mercy upon those who are dying
and upon those who have entered God's rest,
especially _____ and _____.
For this we pray:

+

+

Priest: Merciful God, be close to us
as you were close to Saint Joseph, the husband
 of Mary.
Help us to serve you as joyfully as he did,
so that we may join him in the glory
 of heaven,
for ever and ever. Amen.

March 25

THE ANNUNCIATION OF THE LORD

Priest: In the fullness of time, God announced to Mary
the great dignity of the only Son.
Her heart became radiant
with the dawning light of our salvation.
Let us ask God to pour forth abundant grace into our hearts.

Minister: That God will renew the hearts of all Christians
with the announcement of enduring love,
let us pray to the Lord:

That God will steady the hearts of expectant parents
with the announcement of divine care,
let us pray to the Lord:

That God will refresh the hearts of the poor
with the announcement of speedy deliverance,
let us pray to the Lord:

That God will calm the hearts of those in the shadow of death
with the announcement of faithful protection,
let us pray to the Lord:

That God will cheer the hearts of those who have died,
especially _____ and _____,
with the announcement of eternal life,
let us pray to the Lord:

+

+

Priest: Almighty, ever-living God,
your will for humanity is that none should
 be lost
and that all should be saved in Jesus Christ.
Join our prayers to those of the Blessed
 Virgin Mary,
so that your church may do your will
 faithfully and joyfully.
We ask this through Christ our Lord. Amen.

MEMORIAL DAY
(United States of America)

Priest: Confident that all who have died in Christ
will be raised to life with him for ever,
let us offer these petitions to our
compassionate God.

Minister: For the mercy of God upon our brothers
and sisters,
especially those who gave their lives in
defending our country,
and for their everlasting happiness with all
the saints,
let us pray to the Lord:

For the renewal of baptismal grace in all the
members of the church,
let us pray to the Lord:

For safe travel and enjoyable leisure this
holiday weekend
and throughout the summer months,
let us pray to the Lord:

For the power of Christ's holy cross and
glorious resurrection
that saves us in our need,
let us pray to the Lord:

For the final destruction of sin, death, and
the grave
by the triumph of the risen Christ,
let us pray to the Lord:

+

+

Priest: Holy, immortal God,
give to all who served you in this life
a place of everlasting refreshment, light
 and peace.
Grant that we,
in company with all those who have fallen
 asleep in Christ,
may praise and thank you for ever and ever.
 Amen.

June 24

THE NATIVITY OF ST. JOHN THE BAPTIST

Priest: In company with the great Mother of God,
Mary most-holy,
with John the Forerunner, and with all
the saints,
let us commend ourselves and the whole
world to the mercy of God
in these petitions.

Minister: That, with the courage of John,
Christians dare to proclaim God's Word to
those in need,
let us pray to the Lord:

That, with the self-sacrifice of John,
we give ourselves to generous service of others,
let us pray to the Lord:

That, with the faith of John,
that we trust in the saving power of
Jesus Christ,
let us pray to the Lord:

That, with the humility of John,
we find strength for our weakness
in God's surpassing greatness,
let us pray to the Lord:

That, sharing eternal life with John and all
the saints,
those who have died,
especially _____ and _____,
rejoice in God's salvation for ever,
let us pray to the Lord:

+

+

Priest: **God of holiness,
your hand rested on John the Baptist
and made him a mighty herald for your Son.
As we celebrate John's birth,
help us by his example and intercession
to serve you with heartfelt love.
We ask this through Christ our Lord. Amen.**

June 29

SAINT PETER AND SAINT PAUL, APOSTLES

Priest: In company with Saints Peter and Paul,
who prayed for all the churches of God,
let us confidently call upon their Father
and ours.

Minister: That Pope _____, the successor of
Peter, and all bishops and pastors
will strengthen us in the apostolic faith,
let us pray to the Lord:

That leaders of nations
will protect the church from persecution
and harassment,
let us pray to the Lord:

That those who are suffering
for who they are or for what they believe
will find strength in the Lord
who is at their side,
let us pray to the Lord:

That apostles, prophets, and teachers
will build up this community as the Body
of Christ,
let us pray to the Lord:

That those who have kept the faith in death,
especially _____ and _____,
will rejoice with Peter and Paul around God's
throne for ever,
let us pray to the Lord:

✢

✢

Priest: God of saints and sinners,
by the power of the Holy Spirit
Peter and Paul bore courageous witness
to the death and resurrection of your Son.
Hear our prayer for your blessings,
that we may be more faithful witnesses
to the truth of the Gospel,
the good news of Jesus Christ,
both now and for ever. Amen.

July 4

INDEPENDENCE DAY
(United States of America)

Priest: On this holiday,
we remember that the justice of God is like rock,
God's mercy like pure flowing water.
Let us ask God to take away our sinfulness
as we celebrate God's goodness,
so that we may ask God's gifts for our country
with thankful hearts.

(Select from the following intentions as desired.)

Minister: For a clear message of God's love and power
in the church's ministry of the Gospel,
let us pray to the Lord:

For insight and courage
in federal, state, and local government,
let us pray to the Lord:

For justice and humility, fairness
 and compassion,
in the administration of law
and in the defense of our people,
let us pray to the Lord:

For mutual care and cooperation
and a concern for the good of all
in industry, commerce and agriculture,
let us pray to the Lord:

For wholesomeness and integrity
in art and music, theatre and entertainment,
in sport and leisure,
let us pray to the Lord:

For a vision of social good
and for service to the truth
in every mode of communication,
in journalism and literature,
radio, television, and the Internet,
let us pray to the Lord:

For a deepening of knowledge in the mind
as well as a maturing of the spirit
in family and school and college,
let us pray to the Lord:

For a community that cares in word and deed
in the service of those in need and sickness,
in anxiety and suffering,
let us pray to the Lord:

For everlasting life for those who have died,
especially _____ and _____,
and for all who gave their lives for
    our freedom,
let us pray to the Lord:

+

+

Priest: Great and eternal God,
you have made all the peoples of the earth for
    your glory,
to serve you in freedom and peace.
Give to the people of our country
what they ask of you this day,
so that they may live humbly before you,
devoted to all that is true and good and just.
We make this prayer through Christ our Lord.
    Amen.

August 15

THE ASSUMPTION OF THE BLESSED VIRGIN MARY

Priest: In the assumption of Mary into heaven,
we see the glory that God calls us to share.
As we celebrate the mighty deeds
that God's love accomplished in her,
we confidently ask God to hear our prayers.

Minister: That the church, like Mary,
will rejoice to share Christ's victory
    over death,
let us pray to the Lord:

That world leaders
will ensure that their countries' might
    and wealth
are used for peace and not for war,
let us pray to the Lord:

That those who lift up the spirits
of the poor, the homeless, and the oppressed
will never lose hope in the saving power
    of God,
let us pray to the Lord:

That we who celebrate this Eucharist
will imitate Mary's example of trust and love,
let us pray to the Lord:

That those who have died,
especially _____ and _____,
will find everlasting joy in God their Savior,
let us pray to the Lord:

Let us remember our own intentions.

[pause for silent prayer]

For these, let us pray to the Lord:

✛

✛

Priest: **Mary's God and our God,**
you have blessed us with the gift of your
    beloved Son
and his most-holy mother.
Look with favor upon our prayers
for your continued blessings.
Grant that we, like Mary,
proclaim your greatness in all that you
    accomplish for us.
We ask this through Christ our Lord. Amen.

September (first Monday)

LABOR DAY
(United States of America and Canada)

Priest: God works for our good, now and always.
On this Labor Day,
let us pray for our needs
and those of people everywhere.

Minister: **For the peace and unity
of the holy church of God throughout
 the world,
let us pray to the Lord:**

**For the well-being of the human family,
and for peace among all nations,
let us pray to the Lord:**

**For a just return for human labor
and for a safe environment for all workers,
let us pray to the Lord:**

**For the elimination of slavery
 and exploitation,
and for an end to poverty, sickness,
 and unemployment,
let us pray to the Lord:**

**For the building of a more humane world,
and for deliverance from pain, fear,
 and distress,
let us pray to the Lord:**

For the everlasting joy
of those who have entered God's eternal rest,
especially _____ and _____,
and for the comforting of those who
    mourn them,
let us pray to the Lord:

+

+

Priest: God of work and rest,
we join our petitions to the powerful prayers
of Saint Joseph the Worker.
Grant us what we need, this day and
    every day,
through Jesus Christ, our Lord. Amen.

September 14

THE EXALTATION OF THE HOLY CROSS

Priest: The Lord Jesus humbled himself
and became obedient unto death,
even to death on a cross.
In the power of his resurrection from the dead,
let us pray that all people will be raised up
to new life in Christ the Lord.

Minister: Christ crucified became like us in our weakness;
through his Cross,
may the church become like him in his saving power.
For this, let us pray to the Lord:

Christ crucified became like the poor and the oppressed in their need;
through his Cross,
may they become like him in his triumph over injustice.
For this, let us pray to the Lord:

Christ crucified became like us in our sorrows;
through his Cross,
may all who suffer become like him in his lasting joy.
For this, let us pray to the Lord:

Christ crucified became like us in our human
    lowliness;
through his Cross,
may we become like him in his divine glory.
For this, let us pray to the Lord:

Christ crucified became like the dead in their
    emptiness;
through his Cross,
may those who have died,
especially _____ and _____,
become like him in his fullness of life.
For this, let us pray to the Lord:

+

+

Priest: Lord God,
answer our prayers in your great mercy,
so that the mystery of our redemption in the
    Cross of Christ
may transform us and the world you love.
We ask this through our crucified yet risen
    Savior,
Jesus Christ, who is Lord for ever and ever.
    Amen.

November 1

ALL SAINTS

Priest: Almighty God, out of love for us,
has made us God's children,
and has granted us communion with the
saints in light.
Let us make our petitions with confidence,
for God will give us everything we need
to live as a holy people.

Minister: That the Lord will bless
those who are lowly and poor in spirit,
and be their inheritance for ever,
let us pray to the Lord:

That the Lord will bless
those who are in sorrow,
and be their consolation for ever,
let us pray to the Lord:

That the Lord will bless
those who hunger and thirst for eternal life,
and be their feast for ever,
let us pray to the Lord:

That the Lord will bless
those who search for God with a sincere heart,
and be their vision for ever,
let us pray to the Lord:

That the Lord will bless
those who suffer persecution for
    holiness' sake,
and be their refuge for ever,
let us pray to the Lord:

That the Lord will bless
those who have died believing in
    Jesus' resurrection,
especially _____ and _____,
and be their joy for ever,
let us pray to the Lord:

+

+

Priest: **Ever-living God,
we are gathered as your family
to praise your name and honor your holy ones.
In your kindness, answer our prayers
and the prayers which the saints offer on our
    behalf.
Let us share their communion of life and love,
for ever and ever. Amen.**

November 2

COMMEMORATION OF ALL THE FAITHFUL DEPARTED
(All Souls)

Priest: Blessed is the Lord our God,
ruler of life and death,
for raising the beloved Son as the first-born
    from the dead.
In his life-giving name,
let us pray that all who sleep in Christ
will awake to share his glory.

Minister: The Lord Jesus raised the widow's son to life.
In his name, let us ask God's unending life
for our deceased relatives and friends.
For this, let us pray to the Lord:

The Lord Jesus wept at the death of Lazarus.
In his name, let us ask God's consolation
for all who mourn.
For this, let us pray to the Lord:

The Lord Jesus promised paradise to the
    repentant thief.
In his name, let us ask God's happiness
for all who died in great misery and suffering.
For this, let us pray to the Lord:

The Lord Jesus fed the hungry and healed
    the sick.
In his name, let us ask God's refreshment
for victims of neglect, starvation and disease.
For this, let us pray to the Lord:

The Lord Jesus redeemed his faithful ones
through the cross.
In his name, let us ask God's salvation
for our fellow-parishioners,
especially _____ and _____,
and for all God's servants.
For this, let us pray to the Lord:

✢

✢

Priest: Holy, immortal God,
you are the source of everlasting life
for all your people.
Grant forgiveness and peace
to those whom we remember today at
    your altar.
We ask this in the name of Jesus the Lord.
    Amen.

November 9

THE DEDICATION OF THE LATERAN BASILICA IN ROME

Priest: We are God's building,
the living stones rising on a firm foundation in Christ Jesus.
In the power of the Holy Spirit who dwells within us,
let us offer fervent prayers to the Lord.

Minister: That the church will gather into one
the scattered children of God throughout the world,
let us pray to the Lord:

That believers of all religions
will be able to worship God in freedom and peace,
let us pray to the Lord:

That architects, designers, and artists will use their talents
to reveal the glory of God,
let us pray to the Lord:

That we who render devoted service to God in this Eucharist
will render generous help to our needy brothers and sisters,
let us pray to the Lord:

That all who have died,
especially _____ and _____,
will find a dwelling place in God's eternal
    home,
let us pray to the Lord:

+

+

Priest: Lord God, wise builder of your church,
we ask you to answer the prayers
we have offered in your holy house.
Raise us to share the everlasting glory of your
    risen Son,
Jesus Christ, who is Lord for ever and ever.
    Amen.

THANKSGIVING DAY
(United States of America)

Priest: The earth has yielded its fruit,
for God has blessed us generously.
As we remember to thank God
for the many signs of God's goodness,
let us ask God's blessing upon our world
in these prayers.

Minister: For strength in the Lord's service,
that we may be united in thankfulness before
    our God,
let us pray to the Lord:

For the enduring love
that we glimpse in the ministry of Jesus,
that we may embrace the salvation of our God,
let us pray to the Lord:

For the gifts of the Holy Spirit,
that we may do all that pleases our God,
let us pray to the Lord:

For the healing of the sick, the feeding of
    the hungry,
and the consolation of the afflicted,
that they may know the deliverance of
    our God,
let us pray to the Lord:

For the peace of those who have died,
especially _____ and _____,
that they may celebrate the love of our God,
let us pray to the Lord:

Let us remember our particular needs.

[pause for silent prayer]

For the well-being of our families
and of all who are gathered here,
that we may rest secure
under the protection of our God,
let us pray to the Lord:

+

+

Priest: Giver of all good gifts,
we ask you to accept our thanks
and to hear our prayers.
As you have made our land bear a
    rich harvest,
make our hearts fruitful
with the life and love of your Son,
    Jesus Christ,
who is Lord for ever and ever. Amen.

www.ingramcontent.com/pod-product-compliance
Lightning Source LLC
Chambersburg PA
CBHW051932290426
44110CB00015B/1950